THE
King of the Ants

OTHER TITLES BY ZBIGNIEW HERBERT

Elegy for the Departure and Other Poems
Mr. Cogito
Still Life with a Bridle
Report from the Besieged City and Other Poems
Selected Poems
Barbarian in the Garden

THE
King of the Ants

Mythological Essays

ZBIGNIEW HERBERT

Translated from the Polish
by John and Bogdana Carpenter

THE ECCO PRESS

THE ECCO PRESS
100 West Broad Street
Hopewell, New Jersey 08525

Published simultaneously in Canada by
Publishers Group West, Inc., Toronto, Ontario
Printed in the United States of America

Library of Congress Cataloging-in-Publication Data
Herbert, Zbigniew.
[Essays. English. Selections]
The king of the ants / Zbigniew Herbert : translated
from the Polish by John and Bogdana Carpenter.
        p.   cm.
ISBN 0-88001-618-3
1. Herbert, Zbigniew—Translations into English.   I. Carpenter, John.
II. Carpenter, Bogdana.   III. Title.
PG7167.E64A23   1999b
891.8'5473—dc21   98-6732
                                                             CIP

9   8   7   6   5   4   3   2   1

FIRST EDITION 1999

Contents

Foreword

Zbigniew Herbert is best known for his poetry, and these "mythological essays" might seem surprising. However, they closely reflect the rest of his *oeuvre*, his philosophical and moral concerns as well as his interest in prose forms. From the very beginning of his writing career, Herbert had a sustained interest in prose genres. At the same time, he was interested in classical subjects, Greek, Roman, and biblical. In his earliest poems, figures from the mythological and historical past make frequent appearances.

Herbert's prose works never followed traditional or well-established models. In the 1950s he devised his own unique prose form, what he called "little fables" *(bajeczki)*. These fables were like mock fairy tales, usually brief and written in prose or dialogue form. Frequently mordantly ironic, they satirized a variety of targets. They appeared for the first time in his 1957 volume *Hermes, Dog and Star*, where they formed a separate section. After this volume, Herbert's regular practice was to mix prose poems with unpunctuated verse poems in the same book. Written at more or less the same time, they represented two different ways of approaching similar concerns.

Herbert has also written longer prose essays included in *Barbarian in the Garden* (1962) and *Still Life with a Bridle* (1991). These studies of Western European art and Dutch painting were original in their use of form; they fused—in different combinations—the genres of the essay, the short story, and close personal observation.

As Herbert experimented with new forms in the 1960s, he turned his attention to a type of prose that would permit him to refashion the Greek and Roman classical myths. At first he called these works "apocryphas." He questioned traditional versions and interpretations of so-called "classical" myths with an acutely critical spirit and presented his own radically revised—hence "apocryphal"—versions. Early sketches of these "apocryphas" can be found in Herbert's poetry, for example in "A Parable of King Midas," "The Sacrifice of Iphigenia," and "Jonah."

Herbert has sometimes been mistakenly called a classicist. He has studied his sources thoroughly, but he is by no means an antiquarian. In his prose essays Herbert never simply retells a myth;

instead, he presents a re-creation of it and emphasizes a narrative. The old story or fragmentary text serves as a canvas for a new story that he carries quite far from its original point of departure. It is a springboard for a broader exploration of human behavior. The setting is often a mixture of the ancient and the very contemporary; this procedure is characteristic of Herbert, and can be seen in "The King of the Ants," "The Olympian General," and "The Infernal Dog." The "mythological essay" becomes a twentieth-century philosophical parable.

Most of these mythological essays have been translated from the author's typescripts.

JOHN CARPENTER
BOGDANA CARPENTER

Securitas

At the beginning of the Empire the Romans introduced a new deity to their pantheon. It happened almost furtively, after hesitation and without any theological preparations.

Securitas—this is how she was called—was elevated to the altars and watched over the Emperor's security. But attaching her to a single person, though an important one, deprived the goddess of the indispensable trait of universality.

The sober Romans noticed a contradiction in the nature of the new goddess of Security that was difficult to disentangle, even

1

a seed of conflict. A guarantee of protection by the supernatural powers might lead the Emperor into a state of exaggerated self-confidence, pride, and arrogance. As a rule this is disastrous for the security of the citizens.

A compromise had to be invented. The Romans decided to put another, parallel Securitas for citizens in the heavens. But there were more complications: they had to decide whether it would be one deity with two protective branches, or two separate deities with different spheres of power. If there were two separate deities, what would be their relationship? Hierarchy and division of competence are matters of fundamental importance in any administration, including the heavenly one.

The appearance of the new goddess provoked passionate discussion and a split in popular opinion. The advocates of strong power were delighted by the discovery of the new deity. They thought it was necessary, timely, and at last purely Roman—it put an end to the shameful custom of copying decadent Hellenistic models. They loudly demanded an end to subtle religious disputes, so people's minds wouldn't be confused and their hearts could unite around the new cult.

The republicans—or rather their pitiful survivors—declared they were decidedly (though timidly) in favor of one Securitas for all citizens. They argued that the Emperor was, after all, a citizen too, and it wouldn't hurt to remind him of this at every occasion.

Finally, the fortune-tellers and priests exercised the far-reaching restraint characteristic of conservatives. They limited themselves to elaborating a complicated document and sent it to the Senate. The Senate, in keeping with its tradition, could not reach a decision. It deliberated at length, exhaustively considered all the pros and cons, and after many months postponed answering the important question of one or two protectors of Security *sine die*. No one noticed that on the heavenly field, only the Emperor's Securitas remained.

We do not know the face of Securitas, whether gentle or cruel. Nor do we know her intricate or simple symbols, the ritual, cult, even a single prayer or invocation of her followers. Securitas had the privilege of expressions that were unmarked and unrecorded, of unmeasurable values hovering between zero and infinity. Because of this quality Securitas could penetrate all things, and a moment of inattention was enough for her to become the tissue of our flesh, the backbone of a landscape with a rainbow, the natural order of things.

Only on coins, the oldest dating from the time of Nero, can we see her worn figure: a woman in a chiton holding a spear. Her banal posture and stately immobility are there only to lull our attention. On a small piece of metal it is difficult to express her essence: dog-like vigilance, and furious pursuit.

The victims of Securitas—more precisely, the half-eaten victims—avoided speaking about her. Why should they? The few who had the courage to make their revelations public met with disbelief and a sense of distaste. The conviction is very strong that the misfortune of another reduces, in a way empties, the reservoir of bad fate—that another's bad luck protects us and increases our chances of survival. This salutary illusion always wins over the simple logic of facts. It will be this way forever.

It would be a mistake to think that the constant presence of the goddess was maintained by prophets, priestly councils, and the inspired. Securitas avoided pomp, ostentation, even publicity. She was severe, and content to have faceless executors.

What to call them? The problem appears insignificant but in fact is an important matter, an attempt to define what is the only material proof of the existence of the invisible Securitas. Popular tradition passed on dozens of euphemistic, funny, vulgar descriptions and a whole mine of anecdotes, but this surplus makes the choice difficult. So how should they be called? Functionaries—this sounds very general. Guards—this is full of pathos. Agents—too policelike. We select an emotionally neutral term: Attendants.

The Attendants wait in vain for their Proust. Great art is slow in paying them due justice or crowning their labors. These were countless. Rapt attention, speeding up or slowing down of the pace, sudden turns and pirouettes in a metropolitan ballet, floors, corridors, straining of memory, patient standing at street corners, empty hours in a café with a newspaper read many times over, fitting proofs of guilt together from overheard whispers, bits and snatches of conversation, papers, even from the flies on the ceiling. But these were not reflected, with a hundredfold echo, in any long *roman fleuve*, figurative painting, or opera.

The struggle of the Attendants. Not an obvious one against the enemies of security but a spiritual one, brushing asceticism and even self-abnegation. An inhuman effort of will to erase personal traits, to discard one's own physiognomy—on which the profession left its stamp like smallpox—and to achieve the pure face of a passerby. Only at the moment of attack and boarding, which consists in a delicate or brutal nudge, apologies, entering a conversation about some supposed common acquaintance, vacations in the mountains, participation in an illegal organization—only then will an experienced eye notice how the good-natured face melts away, and the frozen, real face of the Attendant is peering out from under the water. This is all prehistory. In the beginning idyllic, clumsy and awkward, the Attendants move with the spirit of the times and advances in science, carried by the high wave of electronics.

The sadness of the Attendants. Securitas does not lavish warmth on them. Those who have given their entire lives to her ought to abandon any hope of reward. She is a cold and technical goddess whose *potestas* relies on the laws of nature, not the laws of man. Securitas has created a closed system, drawing energy from itself: the old dream of a *perpetuum mobile*. In this system she has introduced numerous bodies which, like planets, circle in marked orbits around a motionless center of power. Changing the system seems as impossible as changing the laws of gravity. The Attendants sense it, and at the same time know they are perfectly interchangeable. A single frown on the goddess's brow and they fall into non-existence. Despite this—or precisely because of this—they serve her faithfully. Indeed, there are many who prefer inexorable necessity to deceptive, dangerous freedom.

Researchers in mythology have devoted far too little attention to the goddess Securitas. Some have maintained she is only a pale personification, but they are profoundly mistaken. What other ancient deity has survived to our own times and enjoys such robust health? This fact alone should be an incentive for deeper studies and for scholarly reflection.

We know that each god ruled over a specific sphere of reality, had his own zealously guarded hunting district and favorite human game. The domain of Securitas is murky, determined by an unclear threat. Her entire inventiveness consists in devising ever-new dangers. She skillfully gives these out in doses, for she knows the art of gradation. Sometimes she is satisfied with a rioting suburb, then she embraces a frenzied city, wanders from one continent to another like the plague, captures land, water, air. Her borders are elastic. Who sets them? Most likely fear.

She does not need temples, sacrificial smoke, processions, or sacred orgies. She is satisfied with a profession of faith in our own miserable physiology. A flutter of the heart, sudden paralysis of the legs, cold sweat, shrieking in a dream—it is not us but our bodies that sing a daily antiphony to her glory.

Securitas belongs to the species of monsters. Compared to her, what are all these childish monster-giants, dragons, half-men and half-animals, hybrids haphazardly sewn together? Securitas is very much like us. She is a monster with a human face.

Like every deity, Securitas draws vital forces from our hopes and fears. She possesses a vast amount of psychological knowledge. She does not lavishly give away eternal youth because this is a charlatan's stock-in-trade. She does not promise other worlds, nor does she deceive us with notions of justice, because when all is said and done each of us—in the depths of the heart—counts only on a final act of mercy. Securitas puts us face to face with the cruel alternative: either security or freedom. TERTIUM NON DATUR.

In our harassed epoch Securitas can count on multitudes of followers. We value security, this lottery in which the winning number is just a stake in a game, a pitiful token that entitles the holder to continue the game as long as the hand continues to serve him.

Security, what is security? A faint-hearted formula for happiness. Life without struggle.

Hecuba

Time—   in every decent epic story it stands aside like a valet, beyond people and beyond objects. Only catastrophes make it leap up from a place, then all of a sudden it forces its way inside with all its destructive power— it breaks, tramples, changes everything to ruins.

Here is Troy—   burning briskly in the crash of collapsing roofs. The time of fire: fast, like wind out of breath, the color of black and red roses. One can hardly hear the moans of the defeated and the victors' shouts.

In the foreground sits desperate Hecuba. A Greek thug has thrown the bloody corpse of her small grandson onto her lap.

Now we expect the cloak binding sky and earth together to be torn by a voice so powerful that—for a moment—everything stands motionless. But there is no voice, just excruciating silence.

Hecuba tears her peplos to shreds, and with tender carefulness her long, agile fingers wrap the little body in bandages, so no blood can be seen, nothing to cause dread. She whispers the name of the boy as she does it, and the whisper, of three repeated syllables, is like a lullaby.

Her rough skin of an old woman has locked itself tightly shut, and she returns to the remote time of childhood, that time of miracles when it is possible to bring every inanimate object to life.

In a moment the slaughterers will come to Hecuba and remove her toy from her hands. Then the kind-hearted gods will transform her into a dog, a bitch, because only the great heart of an animal can contain so much misfortune. Then to find consolation she will throw herself into the sea.

This Horrible Thersites

To Veronica Behrens

The armies took their seats, marshaled in rows and according to ranks. But one man, Thersites, talked on endlessly, full of contention and insults. He baited the kings and looked hard—but in vain—for occasions to sow discord between them, provoking the Achaeans in every possible way and making them burst out in laughter.

A council of the Hellenic chieftains is taking place, disturbed by a strange individual named Thersites. He appears only once in the *Iliad*. In the tumult of battles and quarrels of commanders, his name disappears like a pin in a haystack.

Who was Thersites? According to Homer he was generally despised and had the appearance of a caricature—the ugliest warrior who came to Troy. Lame, with a caved-in chest, a skull warped to a point and covered by scraggly hair. The portrait of a real egghead. His physical appearance was a reflection of his spiritual qualities;

in the poem Thersites is a coward, quarrelsome, and a constant grumbler.

Probing more deeply into the poem, we discover in the episode a wealth of meanings.

There are no background characters in the *Iliad*. The work is a gigantic bas-relief in which there is room only for the heroes fighting against the background of a great plain. If names appear other than those of Achilles, Agamemnon, Diomedes, they are names of those who perished, about whom we know only that they lost their lives at Troy. So why did Homer make an exception for a man with no significance?

The first answer would be that he did it for reasons of composition. Into a stifling atmosphere of blood and violence, he wanted to introduce a comic moment, a *divertissement*, something to provide a moment of respite and pure laughter. But the poem develops inexorably along a straight line toward destiny. It has no detours from the action, comic episodes, or accidental events.

The name Thersites probably comes from a word meaning "arrogant," and this explains his personality. But Homer did not invent the character of Thersites; according to others the name means "brave" and "courageous." It could therefore be a name that carries a comic meaning, in contrast to Thersites' real personality. It is as if the name "Svejk" meant "fearless" in Czech.

Consequently one should not look for the answer to this riddle in onomastics.

Let us return to the poem.

What is Thersites doing in the *Iliad*? He interrupts the council of commanders. He criticizes Agamemnon, asserting that he is using the war to enrich himself, to accumulate conquered bronze and collect pretty female slaves. "Or still more gold are you wanting? More ransom a son / of the stallion-breaking Trojans might just fetch from Troy? / Though I or another Achean drags him back in chains?"

So we are not dealing here with some general grumbling of Thersites, but a completely concrete, material cause for dissent. Does the unjust division of spoils—the captive Briseis taken by Agamemnon—determine the axis of the poem?

Thersites dares to bring charges against the commander not only on his own behalf but on behalf of those who are silent. Therefore he seems to be a voice for the injured.

But who, really, was Thersites? In Homer his social rank is not clear. If he was an ordinary camp follower, he would not have been admitted to the councils of commanders. His name does not appear on the list of ships, so he was not a commander himself. This much we can deduce directly from Homer.

As we said, the author of the *Iliad* did not invent Thersites' name; in other myths he is nothing less than a king of Aetolia, son of Agrios and cousin of Diomedes, a hero of the Trojan War and one of the few who—like Nestor—returned from Troy alive.

Other myths tell that Thersites took part in a hunt for a Caledonian boar that was ravaging the fields of Meleander. A quarrel broke out during the hunt, and Thersites was thrown from a cliff. Thus his repulsive lameness was not inborn but acquired in a fight. Mythology made Thersites a cripple. Indeed he did not deserve the degrading thrashing given by Odysseus in front of everybody in the *Iliad*. Precisely by Odysseus, who was not especially distinguished by bravery, who pretended to be a madman plowing the ocean sand in order to avoid taking part in the expedition to Troy.

How did Thersites come to an end? Homer doesn't mention it. According to other legends, the direct cause of death was a quarrel—again a quarrel—with Achilles.

We know that the Amazons, under the command of the beautiful queen Penthesilea, took part in the last phase of the combat on the side of Ilium. In these battles Achilles mortally wounded Penthesilea—a favorite motif of many painters of vases. A more brutal version of the myth says that Achilles fell in love with Penthesilea's dead body and committed, on the spot, an act of necrophilia. This, on the other hand, seems to be a favorite theme of modernist dramas about love and death.

Thersites rightly ridiculed Achilles for this repulsive action, and the hero, lacking any arguments to defend himself, knocked out all of Thersites' teeth and sent his soul to Erebus.

So much for the myths.

Today we can look differently at Thersites, without Homer's consent. Who was he? A representative of the vanquished, perhaps a Minoan prince stripped of power by the Achaeans.

His only weapon was abuse, the rebellion of the helpless—without hope but precisely because of that, deserving admiration and respect.

The Olympian General

Ares was the son of Zeus and Hera. He was one of the twelve Olympian gods, but it is not clear if this was because of an inexplicable worship of the number "twelve," or some other important reason. He was a second-rate god, auxiliary and generally despised.

The origin of his name was an adjective. Is it possible to imagine a more proletarian provenance?

On a fragment of a ceramic vase from Berlin, we see Ares sitting at the end of a table. He has a perfect resemblance to that unfortunate

13

member of the Buddenbrooks family whose nerves were shorter on one side. Ares was the only neurasthenic among the Olympian gods.

Homer is not kind to him. In the *Iliad* he is a thoughtless fighter, more of a demon for battle. Homer endows him with two distinctive traits: strong legs and a powerful voice. He was unequaled in attack but also in flight. Injured by Diomedes, he screamed like ten thousand men.

The Greek gods were immortal but exposed to wounds, illnesses, and humiliations. Ares received mostly the latter. During the Rebellion of the Giants, he was knocked down by the terrible long-haired sons of Aloeus and put in a bronze chest. After thirteen months he escaped, barely alive, his morale completely broken.

Ares killed the son of Poseidon but refused to admit the murder. He was, therefore, a liar, and this character trait is closely related to cowardice.

Heracles forced him to flee Olympus.

In military science Ares relied mostly on strategy, and the one principle he recognized was the furious attack, followed by an equally furious retreat. In this respect he resembles Napoleon. His opponent was the deliberate Athena, a superb strategist and tactician. She meticulously weighed the odds and never engaged in a chaotic brawl.

Ares would get involved in a war without any ideological motivation. He betrayed often and willingly. He preferred to kill with his own hands. This predilection indicates his barbarian origins. Only the young recruits loved him; they went to war deeply convinced it would be great fun, but never returned to confirm that delusion.

It has been rightly observed that many myths refer to Ares, which means that people liked to say bad things about him behind his back. But Ares had no cult; the temples in his name are rare and meager. Among the Greek gods who possessed academic training and social polish, Ares was indeed a barbarian.

This is how Herodotus described the cult of Ares among the Scythians:

> In each district of the three kingdoms, Ares has his temple. It is of a peculiar kind and consists of an immense heap of brushwood, three furlongs each way, somewhat less in height.
>
> The heap is leveled off on top like a platform, accessible on one side but rising sheer on the other three.
>
> Every year a hundred and fifty wagonloads of sticks are added to the pile, to make up for constant settling caused by rains. In each district an ancient iron sword is planted on top of it, and this is the holy image of Ares.
>
> Annual sacrifices of horses and cattle are made to the sword, which indeed claims a greater number of victims than any other god. Prisoners of war are also sacrificed to Ares, but in this case the ceremony is different from that of the sacrifice of animals. One man is chosen out of every hundred; wine is poured on his head, and his throat cut over a bowl. The bowl is then carried to the platform on top of the woodpile, and the blood poured over the sword.
>
> While this goes on above another ceremony is enacted below, close to the holy spot. It consists of cutting off the right hands and arms of the prisoners who have been slaughtered, and tossing them into the air. When this is done and the rest of the ceremony is finished, the worshippers go away.

The victims' arms and hands are left to lie where they fall, separate from the trunks.

Later, when war became the domain of politics, shabby counselors, and cynical capitalists, Ares lost his standing. He was demoted. The apostle of chaos no longer had the wind in his sails; he aged. But still he made threats—that he was strong, that he could beat anyone in arm wrestling. He drank. He cursed as before.

In the unbearable quiet called peaceful coexistence, what is left for former generals to do? Conquests in bed. Like anyone who has been denied creative capabilities—or at least, industriousness—he contents himself with cheap eroticism. Tintoretto has represented it exquisitely in a painting, *Aphrodite and Ares Caught by Hephaistos*. Naked Aphrodite, a menacing Hephaistos, and Ares under the bed entangled with slippers and a urinal.

At present, Ares has discovered an overwhelming predilection for conspiracies, gangs, and terrorist organizations. His life up to now, and his modest education, have found an outlet in treacherous assassinations and the construction of primitive bombs.

At this moment he is sitting at the terrace of a café, overlooking a quiet city.

He looks at his watch. He pretends to be calm.

Exactly at the designated time, a huge, disgusting rose blossoms in the center of the city. It lasts for a moment. Then one hears commotion and the howling of sirens. Over the spot—the place of execution of innocent people—a black curtain of smoke rises into the air.

Never again will the city be as it was before the explosion.

Ares pays for his coffee, and slowly goes down the steps of infamy.

Endymion

The story is simple and as old as the world. A Great Lady falls in love with a young boy from a lower social class. All the variants of the delicate situation have been sufficiently described by world literature. In this case there is an additional complication: the Lady is the goddess of the moon, and the object of her affection, a hunter. This stunning disproportion in their status augurs nothing good.

Sudden Ionian dusk falls. Tired from a full day of hunting, Endymion lies on the slope of Mount Latmos. Tightly wrapped in the scent of thyme and lavender, he falls into a deep sleep. At the same time Selene makes her routine inspection of the night firmament and notices the small figure, his face trustingly turned to the sky, the mouth open, arms widely spread. Truly he looks like a child fallen from a cradle, and so—overcome by a sudden wave of tenderness—Selene leaves her chariot, approaches the boy, and spends a few unforgettable moments with him.

What a pity it did not end there. It would be a graceful subject for a small bas-relief. Best of all would be a *gemma*, yes, a concave *gemma* cut in onyx which opalizes with pale light, concealing under its smooth, milky surface not a mystery but just a night secret.

The morning after the episode, which insisted on being something more than an episode, Selene appeared before Zeus. After a night excursion of doubtful nature he returned to Olympus, and in a very bad mood was about to settle outstanding business. Paler than usual, Selene could barely control herself.

—I am in love, she confessed.

—That's fine. Quite fine, Zeus said thoughtlessly.

His answer did not measure up to the situation. Zeus knew quite well that Selene—cool, mirrorlike, and distinguished—was the only puritanical goddess. When such people have a love affair they completely lose their heads, and are capable of anything. The matter was serious. It required careful investigation.

—When did it happen? he asked. That is, since when?

—That's unimportant. I know I have always loved him.

—Could I at least know the lucky man's name?

—Endymion.

—Endymion? Never heard of him.

—Endymion, a hunter, Selene explained with pride in her voice that was difficult to understand.

Yes, thought Zeus, it has happened. Once you fall, then you really fall far.

—Endymion, you say. Is he at least well-built?

—He is beautiful, very tender, and certainly wise, although I haven't had a chance yet to find out. We were together only for a moment.

—And this is how it ought to end.

—I don't understand.

—This is how it ought to end. This shepherd of yours . . .

—Hunter. Selene, close to tears, corrected Zeus.

—It's all the same. Remember, and I say this from experience, only fleeting moments have any value. Leave him in peace, if you want to have happy memories.

—I don't want memories, Zeus, I want Endymion.

—Soon you'll find out that Endymion—what a ridiculous name!—speaks nonsense, wheezes like a bull, and is unfaithful to you with some stable girl. An ordinary worm. Grayness wrapped in the nauseating odor of decomposition.

—Can you understand, Zeus, it was exactly his smell that seduced me?

—Smell?

The father of the gods, who was sensitive only to sensations of touch, showed interest.

—Yes, said Selene. I love his smell. Humans call it sweat.

This was a perversion Zeus could not understand. Yet Selene spoke with exaltation.

—You must understand. Endymion carries on his skin the smell of beech leaves, of pine needles, water, heat, sticky buds, ancient moss, the sweet fragrance of raspberries, pungent juniper, the undefinable smell of wing sheaths, bracing acids of ant hills, the odors of animals he kills, the smell of their pelts, blood, fear. And many, many others I can't name. You will say, Zeus, this is nothing special for someone so completely blended with nature by his profession. I agree. But what I am speaking about is merely the surface, the outside of a shell. Inside is the smell of Endymion himself, different from all other smells and impossible to describe. In medicine it is called a characteristic odor.

Zeus listened intently. Here was a back alley of reality bypassed by the gods: aromas and odors. The times had long since passed when the inhabitants of the heavens obediently followed nomads and held on to them tightly, inhaling with flared nostrils the sacrificial odors of burnt meat and tallow. At that time smoke was the only proof they existed, proof of a fleeting affirmation they were necessary until theology and poetry erected more permanent, subtle and irrefutable monuments for them. Now the fragrances on Olympus were indistinct, marblelike, elevated and abstract rather than concrete. To speak plainly they were insipid, without character. Zeus thought: we abandoned the sensations of smell too thoughtlessly. Maybe they have the ability to increase other sensations, so it might be worthwhile to introduce smells that are sharp, exciting, even blasphemous into the palace of the immortals. I must think about it.

Still, there wasn't the slightest doubt that Selene was now beside herself. Zeus dryly said he emphatically forbade any further relations with the young butcher of forest animals. If she wanted to continue her studies of life in lower social spheres, why not widen her investigations and include hat-makers, donkey herdsmen and sailors? They too had a smell. He demanded that a report be made the following morning, at the latest, to definitely close the matter.

Selene left, completely crushed.

Next morning when she reappeared, she was transformed. Bold and clear madness shone in her eyes. Without warning, she declared she could not live without Endymion.

—Think of that, said the father of the gods. She "can't live" without him! But we are Pure Form, Being without alternative, the essence of duration. I can comfort you, however, that what you are experiencing now will be repeated many times in the future.

—That is what is terrible. I yearn for what is unrepeatable and unique, mortal, splendidly finite, earthly and final, whispered Selene.

Zeus was overcome by a powerful, purple wave of royal fury. Before each explosion he couldn't deny himself the pleasure of delivering a small sermon.

—Remember who you are, Selene. Lady of melancholy, of phases and crescents, Lady of long litanies of mists, Lady of waters. This is how people pray to you—a generous dispenser who bestows the cheap jewelry of the sky on everyone. So many matters have been entrusted to your care. You lead lunatic pilgrims on a narrow footbridge between exaltation and the abyss, you move the huge gills of the oceans, you draw the dragnets of the tides. You teach kings the softening of contrasts, that each work of art has to have its own light and be steep like a mirror. How many times have you saved lost wanderers and led the longing arms of lovers toward each other?

At this point Zeus got stuck. He had made a blunder. This was definitely the wrong note to strike; the entire homily was wasted. His words rolled with the force of inertia, beads of images whirled in a circle, and no moral came from it. He was the victim of a disastrously chosen tone. All those silly *affettuoso con tenerezza* completed the devastation. Finally, to get out of the rhetorical tangle, he roared:

—Selene, Selene! Leave the crooked path and return to the way of virtue. After all, you belong to the triumphant church of astronomy. Do you, or don't you?

There was a long silence. Selene said:

—I understand your anxiety. There is only one way out. You must transform Endymion into an immortal.

At this, a dry clap of the thunder rolled over the world.

Selene, who until now had so scrupulously fulfilled her cosmic duties, would not obey. If she disappeared from the scene it would not be too bad. It could be explained as a momentary indisposition, a sudden change of program. A general repair. But who could have suspected the goddess of having resources of black humor, or a sophisticated ability to gradually increase gothic horror? For now a huge shield appeared on the horizon and remained there the whole night, bloody, motionless, lying in wait. Then again the moon glided in a drunken zigzag, frightening hordes of clouds—or it climbed to the peak of the sky and, after a fearful wait, tumbled down like a rock. No voice—and that was the most frightening— accompanied this insane pathology. A leaden silence hung on the heights while dogs howled below, the sea stepped out of its shores, and the stock exchange, that infallible barometer of social moods, sank in delirium.

In some societies the defects now revealed in the sky's mechanics were greeted with enthusiasm, and appropriate conclusions were drawn. A certain wavering of spirit, characteristic of democracies, was transformed into laborious anarchy; and the old nihilism of those who despair was replaced by a new and energetic, vital version that gathered momentum. After a period of joyful destruction and total negation came a period of New Synthesis, which triumphantly proclaimed that truth and falsehood are not contradictory, while crime and virtue, barbarity and civilization, can and should coexist peacefully. Only a few perceived it was nothingness that noiselessly detonated—silent explosions of nonsense shaking the oases of freedom.

In totalitarian regimes vigilance was increased. This meant a shift from painful repression to coldly calculated mass terror. The rulers proclaimed that the blow dealt to a brother by a brother's hand can always be rationalized, and is therefore less painful than the blind, irrational violence of nature. The people were thus steeled for the onset of the unknown. One must bow one's head at the animal patience of subjects. In their collective ecstasies of submission, they reached incredible heights or, if one prefers, the very bottom of degradation.

Poor Python! In vain, completely in vain you left your hiding place to take part in the apocalypse predicted by prophecies. No one even noticed you. Broken and humiliated, you dragged yourself to your depot near Delphi, filled with the bitter knowledge that humanity had matured and become sufficiently monstrous to take the steering wheel of annihilation into its own hands.

Time pressed. One had to act, and act energetically. To bestow immortality on Endymion was out of the question. At that moment Zeus remembered a young scholar, who several times had rendered small but valuable services. Hypnos, yes Hypnos, no one else, only Hypnos could bar the path to raging anarchy.

He was a modest, taciturn young man who studied the phenomenon of sleep. Much later, in the period of decline, he was turned into the brother of death, and a major part in this was played by poets who thought their task was to comfort and tame what ought to remain wild, contradictory, and inconceivable. Equipped with a precise, analytical mind, Hypnos studied dreams as a sickness of the body. This is why he must be strictly distinguished from that gang of imposters, those peeping toms of dreams who subject their helpless followers to horrible exercises and tortures only to leave them in the end without a soul, and in the tatters of the subconscious.

Hypnos understood his task in a flash. Endymion had to be put into a state of hibernation: not so deep that he could not feel external stimuli, and he had to be maintained in this state for as long as possible. Hypnos was an anesthesiologist.

He explained to Zeus—for whom subtle scientific distinctions were foreign—that the mechanics of the sky would be restored to their usual accuracy by immobilizing Selene's lover on the mountain slope so she could continue meeting him at the same spot. The father of the gods was delighted. Selene was ecstatic. No one asked the patient his opinion.

This is what happened. The honeymoon and the following months passed like a dream, in undisturbed harmony, to the joy of both the universe and the lovers. Selene recovered her old equilibrium. She was only a bit more taciturn and pensive.

The fruit of Endymion's and Selene's love was an astronomical number of progeny: fifty girls and as many boys coming into the world regularly every moon-lit month.

And here a gap. Even more, a scandal, criminal negligence of the mythographers. No one knows what happened to the children. Human memory has not even transmitted their names. Yet we are justifiably concerned about the fate of creatures lightheartedly brought to life when we consider that their father was a great sleeper, and their mother roamed at night.

It is easy to imagine this lost centuriate, this abandoned flock—they go by twos, holding each other's hands, always frozen, always rough in the blue-gray uniforms of an orphanage, and with a flaw of injury on their pale faces. The destiny of such creatures is sterile hopelessness. The girls become servants for rich and vulgar bourgeois, and after a full day's drudgery fall asleep in narrow iron beds in a stuffy room without any window or hope. The boys, hungry, cursed and beaten, take any job, and if they are overcome by a moment of rebellion inevitably end in prison. Thus they go in their bluish-gray uniforms, one after another disappearing in a cloud of forgetfulness.

The whole story is full of shadows. What did Endymion feel, granted a luminous love and condemned to misty consciousness? Perhaps he even felt Selene's changes as she approached him: girlish, slender and trembling in the new moon, warm, maternal, insistent in the full moon. One thing is certain: he was attached.

Selene was truly in love. She would whisper magic incantations of love into Endymion's half-open mouth, and was answered by an echo. She was satisfied by the charm of perfect passivity, by the monologue of her own transports and lazy assent.

No one knows exactly when it happened. Selene stopped visiting Endymion. Not a single scene of parting, reproach, or tears. Nothing that shows profound passion: broken china, pumping out the stomach, or at least a slight neurosis. The worst of all possible finales: a sudden attack of strangeness. Like a doll fallen from a carriage, Endymion remains alone on the green slope of Mount Latmos. His open arms embrace no one. On his face, the smile of a country boy who got dead drunk before conscription into the army and fell asleep in the hay. A smile that is intellectually trivial and expressively vapid—simply foolish.

Even his smell that seduced Selene has left him. Now he smells of rain, damp feathers, and artificial sleep.

But he continues to be beautiful. That is, completely useless.

Atlas

I t is difficult, truly, to be reconciled to sky-high injustice.

Consider: The names of Achilles, Prometheus, and Heracles immediately evoke a spontaneous reaction. Because of the pen of Camus, Sisyphus became an allegory of our lives. But about Atlas, not a word. He does not speak to our hearts and minds. He is an exile from the imagination, an outcast of gods and of men. A remarkably small number of sculptures, frescoes, and poems have been devoted to him.

I think the main reason for this neglect is an immobility that is not very attractive; his frozen, silent suffering. Atlas's brother Prometheus, fastened to his rock, splendidly cursed the gods. The one possible action for those who are fettered is speech. Prometheus understood this very well: he moved the ether, and the ether carried the thunder of his curses.

Odysseus, Jason, Theseus, and so many other long-distance runners of mythology became the heroes of dramas. Never Atlas. It was Aristotle who closed the doors of art to him; in the *Poetics* Aristotle remarked that there is no tragedy without action, although tragedy is still possible without personalities.

The whole character of Atlas, his entire being, is contained in the act of carrying. This has little pathos, and moreover it is quite common. The titan reminds us of poor people who are constantly wrestling with burdens. They carry chests, bundles, boxes on their backs, they push them, or drag them behind, all the way to mysterious caves, cellars, shacks, from which they come out after a moment even more loaded, and so on to infinity.

Atlas supports the heavenly firmament. This is his punishment, his curse and profession. No one is grateful to him for it. No one praises him, no one even encourages him. We have become used to it. This is how it should be. We say: someone must do it.

We don't know how he looks. Scholars have devoted so much attention to examining the internal life of the earthworm, the rat, the domestic goose; but they are silent when asked about Atlas's behavior. Does he ever shift his weight? Are his eyelids tightly clenched together? Is the sound from his chest a hoarse breathing, or a moan? Salty drops run down his face: sweat or tears?

Many maintain that Atlas is not distinguished by a lavish imagination, and most likely this deters people—there is nothing sensational. Because we know so little about him, let us state cautiously that cunning, a penchant for intrigue, the hatching of plots and coups d'état were not granted to him by nature. But can we reproach him for this? After all, the structure of the world is woven from contradictory elements that mutually support each other: evil and good, inertia and movement, intelligence and dullness.

What is he thinking? Men sentenced to heavy labor have neither the strength nor desire for thought. With great probability one can suppose that a plan like that of Samson never dawned in the head of Atlas. Samson was put in prison, waited for his sentence, and so had time to forge his revenge. Atlas does not have time. He has only eternity. Atlas endures. Some say, it is good this way.

He managed to free himself from the oppression of fate only once. The story is known, so we will tell it in a considerably abbreviated version.

It was like this: Heracles had to obtain a golden apple from the garden of the Hesperides for King Eurystheus. The garden was not far from the permanent station of Atlas; moreover, the Hesperides were his daughters. Complicated transactions depending on trust are best arranged within the family. Heracles promised to take the place of Atlas during his absence, in exchange for friendly help in getting the desired fruit.

Atlas's journey to the garden of the Hesperides was certainly his most marvelous experience. He walked lightly—a winged column—through a world rid of the burden as if it was made of dew, of azure air, and light. He felt the wonderful weightlessness of all things. For the first time the accursed sky seemed ethereal, distant, and indeed beautiful.

When he returned to Heracles, intoxicated and happy, he naively offered to take the apple to Eurystheus himself. The cunning hero agreed. He asked Atlas to hold the vault only for a moment because he had to shift the pillow on top of his head. It was done—and at this point the unscrupulous hero left the titan. Everything returned to the old cosmic order.

The whole story is not very edifying morally, and socially it is even distasteful. No one knows why it is told to children. Also, it is difficult to understand why the hero of the beautiful metope at Olympia, "Atlas Bringing the Apple of the Hesperides," is the deceitful Heracles, the one who is guilty. He is represented as a handsome man and an athlete, while Atlas, on the other hand, is shown as a rather rough-hewn, clumsy hulk. Implacable time has damaged the metope, and the figure of Atlas has suffered the most.

Later the motif was taken up by generations of architects, and in the temples of Agrigentum, Atlas was given the subordinate role of a cantilever—a male caryatid. His mythological dimension was reduced. Once again he was treated unjustly—it was forgotten, it seems, that supporting the heavens is something completely different from serving as an ornament of a façade. He was given the ambiguous, abject function of holding up balconies and stairs in the palaces of lazy aristocrats and wealthy parvenus, not to mention banks, police headquarters, and ministries of public cruelty.

His solitude is desertlike. Neither day nor night brings him relief. Like all those who fulfill an unattractive duty for a long time, he is beyond the limits of our compassion and understanding. The only companion to Atlas is his burden.

It is not even certain if he would be happy to learn that in a recently discovered Hittite epic, a distant cousin has been found with the sonorous name of Upellura. He, too, carries. This may be verified in reports of the Austrian Academy of Sciences. Unfortunately, these appear in very limited editions and are not intended for manual laborers.

Gods, titans, heroes—O what a fascinating and rich gallery of psychological deviations! Their world swarms with monomaniacs, paranoiacs, melancholics, schizophrenics, not to mention such gentle deviations as alcoholics and erotomaniacs. Against this colorful background, Atlas appears as a faintly etched figure. He is the catatonic of mythology. A catatonic, and a porter.

And yet I think he deserves a better place in human memory. Nor am I certain that he was justly refused the status of a symbol. After all, Atlas represents a very large part of humanity. With minimum good will on our part, and with imagination, he could become the patron of those who are terminally ill, patron of those condemned to life in prison, those who are hungry from birth to death, the humiliated, all those who are deprived of rights, whose only virtue is mute, helpless, and immovable—up to a point—anger.

Cleomedes

Astipalea.

A small island of the Sporades Archipelago southeast of the Peloponnesus—strictly speaking it is two islands connected by a narrow, wet isthmus. Less than a hundred square kilometers of sand, rocks, and scanty vegetation.

What can be said about this place on the earth? Not much, almost nothing. And it is this that seems completely exceptional in a country populated beyond measure with true and legendary history, a country where every cave, forest, spring, and mountain repeats the echo of the gods.

With sadness it must be stated this island was not a cradle of the arts and wisdom, a homeland for explorers of stars, poets, able potters, or even a dynasty of rulers whose picturesque crimes could be the subject of a tragedy. None of its men won fame on the fields of great battles, none of its women were visited by Zeus to become mothers of unpredictable heroes.

Everything here was ordinary, commonplace, flat. Patient sheep trod the summit of the highest elevation called a mountain due to patriotic impulse. The capital: a gathering of pitiful white houses, a noisy agora, a few squat, graceless temples. That was all. Even catastrophes worthy of note, epidemics and earthquakes bypassed the island.

The destiny of Astipalea was, thus, mediocrity. One had to be reconciled to this. Life in the shadow, a quiet recess the storms of history don't reach, all of that has its charm. But although we appreciate our own safety, we hold it against our ancestors if not one had the courage to take part in a dangerous expedition or perish on the field of a famous battle, in a word, if they failed to achieve anything worthy of song.

And so the inhabitants of Astipalea experienced a feeling of shame as they listened to the rhapsodes. Someone even had the mad notion of supplementing the famous catalogue of ships in the *Iliad* to include just one from Astipalea—or of appointing a youth from the island as driver for one of the heroes who struggled at Troy. One can't deny these were modest ambitions. The philologists gently call them interpolations. But at the time we are writing about, the texts of both poems were definitively established, and an attempt to encroach on a past both sacred and fixed would have inevitably provoked jeering. No one in his right mind hesitates when confronted with the cruel choice, eternal ridicule or eternal repudiation.

An obstinate yearning, a collective will working in hiding, untiringly, the hope of many nameless generations that a day will come when the island is born a second time, if only for a moment—all this was fulfilled in a surprisingly simple way. In the family of a blacksmith, a boy was brought into the world and given the name Cleomedes. In this or a similar manner all great tales of humanity ought to begin.

Later the irresistible need for a miracle found prophetic signs and multiplied them: an old oak split on the day of Cleomedes' birth, an eagle could be seen circling above the city. Others spoke of a high tidal wave, of fog assuming shapes of the Olympian gods, a rainbow, and also a strange light that came not from above but it seemed from the center of the earth, transforming this crumb of land into a pale morning star.

The young Cleomedes was meek, quiet, and shy. The gods sent him two gifts that rarely come in pairs and are therefore considered contradictory: beauty and strength. Beauty is a static trait and is inherent—like the beauty of a flower, an ocean bay or a fair summer night. It is content with itself, sure of its own rights, and can ultimately dispense with confirmation, a contest or wreath. The beautiful lead a quiet life and are rarely entangled in dramatic adventures. With strength it is entirely different. Its essence is a challenge thrown to people and to the world. It manifests itself only in struggle, in receiving and administering blows, in a growing pyramid of deeds more and more unimaginable and murderous.

Allow us to interrupt chronology and note that several centuries after the events described here, an Alexandrian versifier slapped together a poem about the youth of Cleomedes the Athlete. Preserved fragments of this inept work can be found in poetry manuals as frightening models of disastrous versification—of stilted pathos and poverty of the imagination—because the author ascribed the deeds of other heroes in the past to his protagonist, ignoring the fact that Astipalea could be the setting of a satirical drama at most, but not of a tragedy requiring pathetic scenery.

After all, no one on this island had ever met a god face to face. The landscape was monotonous, without lions, giants, horses devouring people, monsters of the earth or the sea, tyrants, or even a cleft in the rocks leading to the kingdom of the dead.

Only a single report worthy of confidence says that during a local religious ceremony—a sculpture of marble was taking the place of an old wooden statue of Athena—Cleomedes walked at the head of the procession carrying the huge stone goddess as lightly as an olive branch.

It was decided to send the young man to Sparta, so he could concentrate on thorough studies under the eyes of experienced preceptors. This usually meant training the mind in philosophy and mathematics, as well as acquiring the ability to construct long, ornate sentences and intricate syllogisms. In keeping with his vocation, Cleomedes practiced horseback riding, driving chariots, perfecting himself in the art of throwing the discus and javelin, in running both naked and wearing armor, in the pentathlon, wrestling and boxing.

So he was sent to numerous competitions, provincial to be sure and as a rule ignored by eminent sculptors. This is why we know almost everything about his fate but next to nothing about his physical appearance, because not a single portrait has been preserved of his head, his torso, or heel.

Connoisseurs admired Cleomedes' particular manner of fighting. Always concentrated, and peculiarly devoid of ambition; impersonal, as if submitting to a strange power that led him from victory to victory. He used his energy reasonably, with moderation, conscious it was a favor from fate and, therefore, something given to him with a short lease. His reserves of strength were suspected to be enormous but he drew from them cautiously, so he wouldn't overstep the limits marked out by the jealous gods.

Was he a favorite of the public? In the stadium and theater the audience wants to experience purification through fear and pity, it wants to follow the struggle of passions, blind verdicts of fate, silent defeats and noisy triumphs. Cleomedes, however, invariably carried out a solitary struggle with his own body. The presence of adversaries was indifferent to him, they formed a motionless background and from it the victor would imperceptibly emerge, always surprised, never quite believing it was he and not someone else who deserved admiration and, well, even worship.

A modest hero is an engaging figure, and no one asks whether it is an acquired pose or if the source of such an attitude should be looked for in the deep strata of the soul. What, indeed, is a timid and pale victor? An odd hybrid, an awkward oxymoron, someone carrying an incurable flaw. It seems that Cleomedes' flaw was his complete inability to identify with his own actions. Internally split, somewhat alarming, he was, in fact, frightfully . . . boring.

This is why the famous Spartan athlete Telestes, patron and guardian of the youth from Astipalea, declared that at the approaching pan-Hellenic games, Cleomedes would enter as a boxer, even though he possessed so many other athletic talents auguring laurels. The decision was arbitrary and final. In everything irreversible we have a tendency to see the interference of supernatural forces governing the world—in reality the matter can be completely explained in human categories.

Telestes' intention was simple and shows his discernment in applied pedagogy. For he decided that only in a boxing match would Cleomedes achieve Form, that is, Individual Shape, and at last become someone defined who could be distinguished from others without difficulty or hesitation. For what is boxing? A battle that is open, masculine, even more an allegory of war, a prefiguration of the struggle between life and death. Telestes reasoned exactly that this would force his pupil to mobilize all his dormant forces to answer aggression with aggression, to be rid of his provincial shyness once and for all and become at last a convincing, distinct, happy victor.

Cleomedes' departure for the games was the greatest celebration ever experienced in Astipalea. Almost all the inhabitants of the island gathered at the port. For a long time, noisily and with effusive affection, they said farewell to the future victor (no one doubted it) who would be the first in history to cover their native land with glory.

The opponent of Cleomedes was the famous boxer Hikkos of Epidaurus, who had come close to the victor's laurels twice before at the Olympic Games. This time, sure of victory, he went into the encounter without guarding himself, striking with a huge open hand similar to a stern teacher thrashing an unruly pupil. A fight must be a drama with an epilogue difficult to foresee, a game in which the scales of victory sway; it ought to abound in surprises, tactical devices, stratagems, sharp attacks and lightning-fast returns—meanwhile the spectators were treated to a boring monologue. So they shouted to interrupt the match and send the unfortunate youth back to where he came from, that is, to his shabby island and sheep.

Then Cleomedes proceeded to attack. But it was an attack in his particular style, hardly perceptible, like everything he did—not showy, sluggish in appearance.

The reports by witnesses are contradictory and unclear. They had difficulty in grasping not so much the meaning of the event as its individual fragments.

It was like this. At first Hikkos stood still as if struck by amazement, then he retreated several steps. Some said he looked around helplessly and suddenly toppled over in the sand with his arms outspread. It lasted a very short time. None of the spectators realized what had happened.

The judges of the games were confronted with a difficult task, a fact without precedent that went beyond the power of judgment. For a dark image concealed everything, and images obstinately resist the efforts of interpreters. Here in full sunlight, in the middle of the arena, something heavy was lying enclosed in itself, soaked in mystery—an object. This is why the verdict of the referees is marked by frightened helplessness.

It was confirmed first of all that Cleomedes didn't transgress any of the minutely established and strictly observed rules of combat. His adversary had not raised his right hand: the sign of surrender. And yet Hikkos had died. Hikkos was not alive. Cleomedes was cleared of the charge of intentional manslaughter, but was refused the victor's wreath. Therefore the duel was unresolved.

The intention of the judges can be considered understandable, morally irreproachable, praiseworthy. But from the point of view of logic, their reasoning was full of gaps, inconsistencies, and contradictions, for no one established what should have been the first and fundamental premise, that is, the cause of Hikkos's death. Can the accidental death of a participant be excluded? A poet who has died over an unfinished poem stirs generous understanding in the hearts of women and even of critics, so why refuse these tender sympathies to boxers? Further, if Cleomedes fought honestly and was judged to have no blame, why was he punished? Finally, wasn't this rather unfortunate phrase about a duel with no victor a cowardly attempt to overthrow the laws of fate, which always decide irrevocably and cruelly—it was also true in this case—leaving only the defeated and the victor on the field?

Cleomedes was plunged into sorrow and despair. He rejected the world, which he had never understood anyway. Therefore, perhaps the rejection was not a great one. On the other hand, it was fraught with consequences.

It was foreign to the ancients to rummage in the labyrinths of individual souls, and they would have said his reason was darkened by the sinister goddess Ate, disturber of the minds of gods and men. For believers, such an interpretation is sufficient. But when we describe what followed, we will try to avoid psychology as well as lofty symbolism and limit ourselves to a simple presentation of the facts, as with Pausanias who first recorded the story.

So Cleomedes returns to Astipalea. He sets out in the direction of the city. A school building is next to the road, and the madness of the unfortunate Olympic athlete is vented upon it. The wooden columns collapse. Under the rubble sixty children find their death.

The inhabitants of the island want to inflict punishment on the criminal at the place of the crime: that is, to stone him to death. Cleomedes succeeds in tearing himself away. He flees to the temple of Athena. The relentless crowd pursues him.

In the temple is a stone chest, as large as a royal vault and reserved for the storage of sacred objects. Cleomedes pushes aside the heavy lid and slips inside.

At just that moment the avengers appear in the temple. They carefully look at every bend of the wall, every nook and cranny. Nor do they overlook the huge stone chest. In vain, Cleomedes has vanished without a trace.

When we read the story by Pausanias we instinctively feel a disquieting lack of a point, a moral, a . . . bottom. The protagonist suddenly leaves the scene and sinks from sight without a word. The Messenger and the omniscient Chorus who bring the voices of the world to the scene are silent about his fate. It is exactly this that glaringly contradicts the fundamental laws of classical drama and, even more, any art expressed in closed and understandable forms.

In the Theater of the Absurd, Cleomedes could have counted on quite a career. Only a chronic lack of education in the men of letters working toward the multiplication of chaos explains the astounding fact that they have not discovered this golden vein; they would have a ready anti-hero of flesh and blood, not watery words, also a subject shimmering with the dark colors of the absurd.

Returning to the interrupted plot: we must emphatically stress what is essential, namely, the close kinship of Cleomedes with the elements. He was a modest athlete and didn't know very well what to do with his great gift. He understood that nature had endowed him with strength that neither he nor anyone else knew how to master. Mastery is not the domain of genius but of barely capable individuals who possess the art of imitating passions and safely balancing over the abyss. Cleomedes lacked this ability. It is why the tale about him takes place on the frontier between human affairs and the phenomena of nature. Down the steep slope of a mountain, or a narration, crushing everything in its way, rolls a boulder. Only ruins and victims remain. But catastrophes after all are innocent.

The bottom, the true bottom of the story of Cleomedes was absolutely real: several decaying planks on the floor of our hero's hideout that collapsed under his weight. He crashed through. He recovered in a dark interior similar to a small, damp cave.

The temple of Athena stood on a hill near the sea. The city had no defenses, but we know that wars and even pirates bypassed miserable Astipalea. It is hard to say why those who erected the temple dug a subterranean passage under the foundations that was soon forgotten.

For a long time Cleomedes crawled in darkness. When he came out at the shore it was night. He found a boat, and the loud sea carried him away.

Cleomedes' wanderings abounded in all the necessary elements of an epic tale: intricate adventures, labyrinths of deserts, summits and depths, terror and vast landscapes. But a sinister shadow followed him that shattered the meaning of his sufferings and struggles, ravaged his being from within, and pushed him deeper and deeper into the domain of inhuman creation. Who was he? An atom wandering in the void of the universe.

Our loyal compassion has accompanied the peregrinations of Odysseus for centuries; this is because the wanderings of the King of Ithaca have supernatural and, at the same time, human dimensions. They move heaven and earth, envious and friendly gods, sirens, monsters, and the hearts of listeners. But the true source of our empathy is the simple fact that all the torments and blows falling on the hero were the price paid for the return to his homeland. Cleomedes' road runs in exactly the opposite direction—he was running away from his beloved island where only a stony death awaited him. He was a deserter from fate.

Finally he reached Corinth, and decided to remain for some time because the feeling of fear left him—not completely but sufficiently for him to recover. He didn't choose this place for its attractions, but simply because ships from different parts of the world landed here and, therefore, news of his beloved Astipalea would reach him, news bringing forgiveness or damnation forever. Even if this did not happen, it was the most suitable place on earth where one could disappear for the second and final time.

The would-be Olympic victor joined the royally hospitable and voluminously bottomless class of ancient proletarians. They were different from slaves because they were not offered for sale, therefore the price of their lives and drudgery was not measurable. The adjective "ancient" is not a decorative epithet but a definition of a place in time. The face of extreme poverty is always, everywhere, equally immovable and repulsive.

He was living, then, in a crowd of the poor cooped up under a naked sky or in wretched mud huts beyond the limits of the splendid city, in an area of abandonment without frontiers. Fires would burn here long into the night, the small lights looking like those of a large, weary, besieging army struck by inertia. Even wakefulness and sleep are not justly distributed among people.

Cleomedes worked by the sweat of his brow. He carried clay to ceramic workshops, sometimes he was employed at the ovens casting the famous Corinthian bronzes, but mostly he worked in the port, an evil, noisy arena of deposed athletes. The city—wealthy, licentious, and huge—lay beyond the borders of his curiosity.

So the groove of his existence was desperately narrow: from the hovel where he slept, to work, and back, that's all. Above his head he had immeasurable time, homogeneous as the air and, like air, without promises. The earthly fate of Cleomedes was fragile, and perhaps for that reason he felt safe in the universe. Degradation gives certainty. There is no better hiding place, no better hospice, than the bottom.

The main concern, or to speak loftily, spiritual occupation, of Cleomedes was waiting. The goal of waiting was to return to Astipalea. He knew it would happen when the witnesses of his crime had died out and as a reward for his patient fidelity, fate would favor him with the gift of death on his native island, ordinary and innocent as birth.

In the beginning he asked all the sailors he met if they had happened to land on the shores of Astipalea. The majority didn't even know the name. Some had seen it from a distance—a dark stone projecting above the surface of the water. Soon Cleomedes gave up his investigations. His simple philosophy was based on reasoning similar to the manner of thinking of lovers, that is, without logic: I am an inseparable part of my land, we were violently separated, if there is any order in the world our incomplete existences must be brought together again.

How could Cleomedes' state of mind be described? We know little about his inner life. But it seems that obvious and worn-out designations like "homesickness" and "nostalgia" can hardly be considered accurate in the case of a protagonist whose nature was marvelously uncomplicated and therefore escaped analysis.

In one of their hermetic texts, the Pythagoreans warn against "eating one's own heart." It should be understood figuratively as a prohibition against sinking into fruitless despair. We can suppose that despite sensible advice, Cleomedes fed himself with his own heart—and it was continually restored, beating strongly with a healthy, hopeless, filial attachment.

He was patient, concentrated as always, enclosed within himself, and self-sufficient. He humbly submitted to the powerful force of time. He well knew that hard labor, the flogging of frost, rain and heat would finally change his skin, furrow deep clefts in his face, bend his back, and give him an uncertain, wobbly step. Then he would be able to return safely to Astipalea. He was waiting for the torn costume of an ancient vagabond from nowhere.

If he had worries, there was only one: he was aging too slowly. In spite of the laws of nature and his own efforts, he still resembled the youth who departed on that memorable morning for a victor's laurels.

Years passed.

Modern poetics rejects similar sentences with disgust; they are just as suspect as, for example, a statement that "the last rays of the setting sun fell on an old house hidden in the shade of centennial lindens," or, "the shapely breast of the countess Julietta was shaken by strange sobs." Aesthetes say they are ugly and banal. That may be. But is it fitting to decorate matters that are profound and ordinary—that is to say, universal—with the artificial flowers of style? And so, years passed.

Chance—the other side of the coin conventionally called necessity, or its capricious variation, horribly unsystematic and absent-minded—chance caused our hero to meet quite unexpectedly in the port a man who had seen Astipalea with his own eyes and was there not long ago. Cleomedes was delighted and invited him that evening to his fire.

The man's name, Heliodorus, should be interpreted as a pretentious pseudonym attached to a small, active, sweaty figure condemned to the eternal torment of throwing out of himself an unending number of words and sounds. Those who have been in the Piraeus and seen the sellers of fortunes know what this is.

By profession he was a wandering peddler of devotional objects. When business in this line weakened or became disappointing, he was also an unlicensed poet. There is no contradiction in this. Both these professions have gone hand in hand for thousands of years.

An inventory of Heliodorus's jumble of odds and ends: Egyptian (or facsimiles of Egyptian) amulets, Babylonian love elixirs, clay figurines that caused sudden death to a hated person when pierced with pins—or, if it was desired, a long and painful one. He also interpreted dreams. He always explained them to the advantage of the dreamer (little caring about the subconscious, that idol not yet invented) because he knew that people crave comfort.

He treated the world as a phenomenon with a certain shade of indulgence and even contempt. He thought it an absurd joke of the Demiurge, and foretold its approaching end. This also comforted those who despaired. And he was an execrable poet. At this time the art of the wandering aodists was in complete decline; the few who had something to say recorded their thoughts and stanzas on papyrus rolls.

So they met at night and, either from his heart's need or perhaps giving in to the prompting of naive cunning, Cleomedes asked Heliodorus to describe Astipalea as accurately as he could. His description agreed exactly with the real topography. Our hero was calmed, dreamy—he made himself a comfortable place near the fire and covered himself with a coat. Tales that grow from the earth are best listened to in a lying position.

The rhapsode moved along smoothly, apart from a number of obstacles typical of the genre such as literary devices, recurrences, descriptions of nature, retardations, and moaning apostrophes to the Olympian deities. Aside from these everything was true: the mysterious death of Hikkos, the hecatomb of the children, the chase, the escape to the temple. Then came the turn for the second part, and as Cleomedes listened about Cleomedes he was plunged into a story he didn't know at all.

From the hoarse, epic tale of Heliodorus, we will try to pick out only the essentials, the mood of the crowd, and the facts.

This is how it was. When the inhabitants of Astipalea discovered beyond any doubt that Cleomedes had disappeared without a trace, like a dissolving cloud, they were struck by an astonishment so great it took away anger and the desire for revenge. It was not the naive, human astonishment we experience at the sight of a calf with two heads or falling stars, but something leading to the depths, and toward the threatening abysses of final matters. The color of the crowd's feeling became darker, the anxiety turned to fear, fear became terror. A great covering of mystery stretched over the little island. Everyone waited for the end and believed that the deluge, pestilence, fire, and beasts were standing at the gates of Astipalea.

In fact, all that could be observed—and that nothing could explain—was a metamorphosis of light. Nothing dangerous on the surface, as long as the sun's chariot rolled along its ordinary path. But now the inhabitants of the island were sensitive to every change, and they fearfully noticed every occurrence that seemed to go beyond the sphere of admissible normality.

Here in the middle of a moonless night, small lights started to emerge from under the earth, and crept low to the ground, blinking on and off. Almost each day brought new signs. Everyone commented on a certain sunset stripped of any transparent burning red, a sunset completely yellow like saffron—then a pale dusk lasting too long, a silent, tall, hard twilight suddenly giving way to basalt darkness as if cut off by an ax. Even at noon, when the sharp light rang down from above, scaring away all half-shades and spectres of colors, one could see the flight of hardly noticeable clouds dragging behind them on the earth hues of lead, hues of heavy crimson, of ash.

All this was associated with the sudden departure of Cleomedes and portended, unavoidably, approaching catastrophe. Thus at night processions went by the light of torches along the flat shores of Astipalea, carrying prayers to the immortal gods: that plagues be diverted, and that he who had disappeared so absurdly should return to his homeland, for his sins had been forgiven.

Because these and other rituals had no effect, it was decided to send a few frightened citizens to the oracle at Delphi. Heliodorus described the navigation at great length, multiplying the dangers and adventures beyond any need. For this, let him be forgiven. He succumbed to form, and form often devours content.

It is universally known that the oracle expressed itself in an intricate, opaque manner. This not only failed to diminish its authority, on the contrary it raised it. After all, the language of the eternal ones must differ from the language of mortals. This can be explained also in a down-to-earth manner: man cannot endure a naked, self-contained, silent mystery. If it is accompanied by words, especially those that are dark and extremely disheveled, it becomes easier to bear.

This time the voice of the oracle was clear, unambiguous, and emphatically articulated. Heliodorus made a solemn pause, then pronounced this divine couplet, recorded by Pausanias.

Cleomedes of Astipalea—last of the line of heroes—
Is immortal therefore pay him due honor.

Thus the story. It ends with the most elevated chord that can be imagined, namely an assumption.

Heliodorus didn't neglect to boast he saw with his own eyes the monument raised to the glory of Cleomedes by the inhabitants of Astipalea. The statue was huge, somewhat bulky, and represented a young man with his hands stretched lengthwise along the body, his fists clenched, and with a mysterious smile, the left leg set slightly forward. Every year on the day of his miraculous disappearance, sacrifices of young sheep were placed at the base of the monument.

Heliodorus fell silent. He was waiting. Like all authors, he was waiting for praise. The man for whom the tale was destined lay motionless on his back, and did not reveal the least emotion.

The wandering poet bent over him. He saw a face in which it was impossible to perceive the majesty of death, or any majesty at all, rather a helpless, blunt, frozen astonishment.

Heliodorus covered the head with a coat and went to the nearby fires of neighbors, for he knew that poor people crave comfort.

Antaeus

Antaeus was the son of Poseidon and Gaea. To put it gently, not a very harmonious couple. What else could be expected from the elements of sea and earth, fighting each other fiercely? It is probable that Antaeus was a neglected, abandoned child—but how difficult it is to imagine the childhood of a giant! The savage quarrels of his parents certainly had a negative influence that shaped his character.

All sources agree that Antaeus grew up to be a crude, violent man, with more than human strength. His intellectual resources were modest, but his body was exuberant. Although he never went to any school, he drew a logically correct conclusion from this disproportion: he became a sportsman.

It is difficult to place Antaeus on the map of the world. In the old myths his home was Libya, it was there that he met Heracles. But later, with Greek colonization of the northern shore of Africa, this fairy-tale-like figure was pushed farther west, all the way to Mauritania where Punic merchants drove the Greeks away. Colonizers do not create myths, but instead labor tirelessly on their geography. They simply locate monsters on terrain occupied by their competitors. This procedure has survived commendably to our own times.

We know little about Antaeus himself, except that he was nourished with the meat of lions he killed with his bare hands. He scorned modern civilization—the cudgel, the spear, the trap dug in the ground. His favorite occupation was challenging wanderers he met to a wrestling match. The adversary was forced to fight, and these struggles inevitably ended with his death.

Such a way of life cannot awaken our sympathy or our approval. But a poet—this is unusual—hurried to Antaeus's rescue. The eminent poet Pindar defended him from the accusation he was simply an ordinary assassin, a repulsive murderer. In one of his *Isthmian Odes*, Pindar tried to discover a meaning in the criminal activity of Antaeus, or at least to make it comprehensible.

The region where Antaeus lived was poor in stones, and only the wind sometimes erected deceptive monuments of sand. Imaginary cities of marble sometimes appeared on the dry horizon. Pindar wrote that Antaeus dreamed of erecting a temple to honor his father. He humanized Antaeus, and endowed him with the praise-worthy virtue of filial love. The only solid materials at his disposal were the terrestrial remnants of his unfortunate adversaries; there was nothing to do but take advantage of this building material. The idea—rather macabre in itself—is not, after all, so far removed from baroque aesthetics.

So Antaeus collected the bones of those he killed just as a good builder lovingly collects stones, bricks, and wood. He took care to preserve them safely from the sun, the omnivorous sand, and humidity.

He changed the plan of his edifice many times. He wanted the mausoleum honoring his parents to have the ideal proportions of the human body.

The apses were made of ribs, he also used ribs for the temple's vault. Beady wrist bones hung down, creating an illusion of lamps and chandeliers.

The columns were made from the bones of spines. He tied several together to give necessary strength to the building.

Each year, during the season of winds and rains, the temple would collapse. All the builder's labors recalled an abandoned camp of hyenas. Bones lay in disorder on the sand. It was as if the gods sneered at those who try to become higher, destroying them.

And every year Antaeus began anew with the same stubbornness, piety, and hopeless love.

Seen from a distance, and illuminated from above, Antaeus resembled a boulder slowly moving through the wilderness. His gait was like the mannered way actors move in Westerns, but in the case of the giant it was a hard necessity, not a mannerism. He drew all his energy and strength from the earth—from physical contact with rock, with clay, even with dust.

If he were not a child of the gods—no one dared question this— one would think that nature treated him unfairly, refusing him a definite spot in the chain of being in a moment of distraction. Who knows whether the form of a tree, a cedar for example, would not be the most appropriate shape for his existence. But Antaeus was an above-ground creature; he was deprived of roots, and marked by fear of the abyss of air surrounding him on all sides. The birds and stars suspended above filled him with revulsion. Each jump or leap made his head turn, and he would feel faint.

Antaeus did not have a home or permanent stopping place. Nights in the desert fall fast: the gray lightning of dusk, and then— right away—darkness. When the sun was about to set, Antaeus would build a shelter: a deep underground corridor so narrow there was only room for his supine body. He would squeeze into this murky, humid refuge like a huge worm, falling into blissful, nourishing sleep.

One can explain these nightly practices of Antaeus symbolically, as a nostalgic search for origins or a return to the mother's womb. But why multiply hidden meanings when everything can be explained in a simple way: by cycles of vegetation.

Everyone who has been in the dessert has noticed clumps of twigs and leaves that appear completely dead, rolled by the wind. At first glance they seem like the trash of creation, crumbs from Mother Nature's table. But as soon as the first rains come, a sudden metamorphosis takes place. What seemed to be forever thrust away from life sends down roots, blooms, intoxicates with fragrance, bears fruit—in a word, lives wonderfully in a powerful, lavish way.

There are reasons to believe that the encounter between Antaeus and Heracles was accidental. This is why it was not engraved on the bronze tablet that describes the main labors of Heracles. It was not planned on the hero's calendar—well, it was one of his guest performances.

All sources agree about the results of the duel, but the way it took place has been reported differently. Diodorus Siculus describes it as a wrestling match combined with a wager that required the loser to forfeit his life. (But he does not say if it was by his own hand or that of the victor.) This is a flat, vulgar version, bringing to mind the rules of gladiators' fights or—even worse—Russian roulette. Other accounts, not very edifying either, say that Heracles blocked the entrance to the underground refuge with his own body, what might be called "starving out the city."

Antaeus was humanized not only by Pindar but by Plato himself, who endowed him with professional intelligence and the invention of certain wrestling grips. Thus poetry, time, and philosophy all labored to endow the fight with the features of a real *agon* in which adversaries had statistically equal chances.

In reality it was an open, manly duel: *mano al mano,* and murderous.

Heracles understood right away that he was engaged in a fight without precedent. Battles and wrestling matches are based on the attempt to deprive the enemy of an upright position—to reduce him to a supine object. But each time Antaeus was thrown on the

ground he sprang up more and more vigorously, ready and rau-
cous, aggressive.

The hero had to abandon normal tactics. He had to overcome
the concept, deeply rooted in us all, of what we call high and low,
the elevation of the victor and the throwing of the defeated down
into the dust. For every time Antaeus was lifted up, it meant death
for him.

Literary accounts of the encounter are few and this is why it is
difficult to recreate the course of events. By their nature, mosaics,
sculptures and paintings record a moment, not a sequence of
events. I believe that the content of the duel—its raw essence—was
best represented by the Renaissance painter Antonio Pollaiuolo.
His painting is small, almost a miniature that can be covered by the
hand, but has such an amount of pent-up energy that its power of
expression surpasses yards of garrulous frescoes.

Pollaiuolo did not succumb to the temptation of presenting Antaeus as a giant. The rules of humanism forbade such expression-
istic whims, so both adversaries have human proportions. They
also lack classical beauty; instead they are a well-matched pair of
similar broad-shouldered, long-haired savages. This was an accurate intuition, for in reality the duel was brutal, its ending naturalis-
tic, ordinary, without a trace of noble simplicity or quiet greatness.

The hands of Heracles tighten around the hips of his adversary
like iron clasps. Similar to a peasant with legs apart, struggling with
a sack and trying to lift it over his back, he tears him from the
ground and raises him to the level of his shoulders.

Antaeus no longer defends himself. He presses his clenched
fists against the elbows of Heracles—he throws his head back,

drawing his legs up. His helpless defense recalls a big fish thrashing in a net, flinging his entire body backward and flinging it forward, until the pendulum becomes completely still.

His mouth is wide open, but he does not shout. Asthmatics, breathing in crumbs of air with difficulty, do not waste strength on screams and curses. In a moment, it will be the end.

Heracles will carefully wait for the moment when his adversary's arms fall along the body and his legs dangle limply like the legs of a hanged man. Then he will listen attentively to Antaeus's silent heart. With relief he will throw the burden to the ground. For a moment he will stand above him. Perhaps he will think with a bit of melancholy that Greek mythology does not know the word resurrection.

Yet Antaeus keeps returning. He strives after our memory. No longer savage and elementary but devoid of violence, almost nostalgic.

In upper Egypt Antaeus was given the posthumous title of a god. A city was baptized in his name. Who would have thought that from a chthonic monster, he would be completely transformed into an apostle of civilization and the middle class?

A mound was discovered near the Mauritanian city of Tingris, and it was generally believed that the terrestrial remains of the giant lay underneath. It was a tomb but also a place of witchcraft. It was enough to dig up some dirt from the topmost layer, and it would produce atmospheric precipitation. An amazing career indeed—from a brigand to a conjuror of rain.

It is possible to risk the assertion that the meaning of the myth of Antaeus is attachment. It is a feeling rather than an ideology, and surely this is why it is impossible to communicate it to others. It is extremely difficult to convince someone that it is worthwhile to love a meager plot of land as small as a donkey's shadow, as the shadow of a poplar, a broken house, or a destroyed city on a dried-up river. In a word, the place where we were born, and which was unable to feed or protect us.

For the nomads of civilization and the tenants of jet planes, Antaeus will remain forever the symbol of a primitive barbarian. They succumb to the illusion that the breaking of ties and a sickly mobility are necessary conditions of progress. But they forget that chasing after the sun and global utopias must end in catastrophe. In the last analysis everything is reduced to the choice, or the assignment by others, of a place in the cemetery.

All those strange refugees who take on the shapes of incomprehensible mutants or even monsters in the pitiless eyes of the natives will find gracious shelter in the shadow of the outspread arms of Antaeus.

They have saved only two minute treasures—their own speech, and names that sound in foreign ears like the bells of a clown. Their land was snatched from them as well as the water in which they saw the faces of their god and of the invader.

Now they are silently dying in the thin air of freedom that belongs to others.

The Infernal Dog

Surviving records about the anatomy of Cerberus, and his physiological as well as psychological functions, are numerous but show alarming divergences. The ambition of the present study is to throw a new shaft of light on a muddled problem.

According to the Archpoet Homer, Cerberus was simply a dog. Dante calls him a worm. Hesiod mentions Cerberus twice in the *Theogony*, but is unable to decide if he has one head or fifty. Pindar doubles this number, while Horace endows Cerberus with a mane of snakes. The tragedians are more restrained, content with three heads. Sculptors and painters represent Cerberus with three heads at most. Here an observation comes to mind—language is inclined to hyperbole and exaggeration if not lying, while a statement in marble or paint imposes a matter-of-fact simplicity.

Because of the dim illumination at the place of action, the outcome of the struggle between Heracles and Cerberus—guardian of the kingdom of the dead—was unclear. It was the twelfth, the last and most difficult, labor of the hero. Hence the sacred semi-obscurity that befits other worlds.

What kind of a fight was it? It is impossible to form a clear opinion based on the literary excavations; different, contradictory versions vacillate between a bloody wrestling match and something like a Sunday hunt for booty. Some say it was Kore who gave Cerberus to Heracles as a gift, just as parents might give a bicycle to a boy for good behavior. Others claim that Hades, ruler of the underworld, was mortally bored and arranged something like a tournament. But the animal and the man wrestled with each other—long, and painfully.

A question remains: what was the character of Cerberus? Demonized beyond measure, he played the decorative role in Hades of a doorman in front of a hotel. The number of the dead who wanted to return to earth was insignificant. Cerberus was not overworked. He was like a sign, BEWARE OF THE DOG and NO EXIT. What kind of a demon was it that could be bribed with a honeycake? His threatening function was to wag his tail.

Whatever happened, neither adversary was wounded. Hence the conclusion that it wasn't a battle in the strict sense of the word but a strategic maneuver, circling the adversary and forcing him into unconditional capitulation. Most likely Heracles used the classical method of strangling. But this is a detail. It is enough that the breathless hero surfaced—together with his prize—above the ground.

It happened . . . exactly where? Again sources vacillate, mentioning a number of points on the world's map. But the problem is academic. We know from experience that in every mature civilization, descents to hell are numerous. Even more numerous than beer stands or mailboxes.

In hell Cerberus barked with a powerful voice. On a mute amphora in the Louvre, the painter Andikos has seized the significance of the duel between Heracles and Cerberus: Heracles assumes the position of a runner at the start, the body thrust forward, right hand moving in the direction of the beast's forehead, a huge chain in his left hand. Cerberus is two-headed. One of the heads is watchful and aggressive, but the other bends to the ground as if awaiting the man's touch. Such is the beginning of the tragedy called taming.

Cerberus is the victim of the assault. How does he feel? The initial light shock has already passed and now another shock begins, so strong, so overpowering that it threatens the dog's heart. He is like a deepwater fish dragged onto the sand.

Sounds, shapes, odors fall on him like an avalanche. The world appears in furiously intense colors like Fauvist paintings: the grass flaming red, trees cinnabar, limestone rocks violet and black, the sky green. Only Heracles has a gentle hue, his figure surrounded by a delicate, pulsating contour.

Harder to bear is the deluge of five hundred thousand odors.

The fiery sun over the dried-up earth.

Under an oak tree, on a high hill, a dog and a man are lying next to each other.

They do not take their eyes off each other. They are distrustful rather than hostile.

Heracles smells of blood, leather, and slaughter; Cerberus smells of decomposing proteins. They belong to two irreconcilable worlds.

Suddenly it occurs to Heracles that if Cerberus wants to leave him, he cannot prevent it. He decides to speak. In such cases the sound of the word has a captivating force.

Heracles: Listen to me, beast. You are my prisoner. If you try to escape, I will smash your head—heads, he corrects himself—according to international law.

Cerberus gives a prolonged growl.

It is night now. There is a big moon.

Cerberus rises on his hind legs. Heracles reaches for his blood-stained club.

At this moment a song is heard. There is little sense in describing music—only those who have listened to the voice of a wolf on a snowy plain during winter nights can conceive of the cantata of Cerberus. For those who have not experienced this wonder, we give a rough transcription of the original, as inept as a newspaper reproduction compared to an original Rembrandt. The following paraphrase is from Alexander Schmook, *Der Wolf—sein Wesen und seine Stimme,* Tübingen, 1848:

Hurr hau - u- uh
hau hau
U - i - jaur - huuu
Ho hau
Hurrrrr ho hauuuh
Jau jau ho hurrr hau - uh

Resounding silence, then repetitions at equal intervals of time.

Heracles is carried away by Cerberus's voice as if on a powerful ocean wave. As he listens he wants to howl with him. But he knows he would discredit himself, for he is unable to draw such pride and despair from his throat. In vain would he try to describe with his voice the chains of land, abysmal spaces, the innumerable springs of blood hidden in bodies of animals, secrets of water and thirst, the hiding places of light and immense blackness.

The road leading to King Eurystheus, who was to free Heracles from his curse, was long. Cerberus began to be attached to Heracles. His character of a monster underwent a metamorphosis—he became like a dog.

People of a sentimental disposition might discover something moving in this. But the hero had a temperament devoid of feeling yet impulsive at the same time. He noticed that whenever he raised his head, Cerberus did the same, and a barely restrained fury grew in him. The dog became the mirror of his master, a distorted mirror, we should add, because of the difference of postures.

But the worst was yet to come. Cerberus began to speak. Awkwardly at the beginning, with much saliva, he would pronounce words like "myum" or "beddy," but his vocabulary became richer from day to day, his syntax more complicated.

Especially at night, Heracles forgot he was wandering with a dog. He kept his feelings in check, remembering that his role was to guard a captive.

Heracles: I don't like you. I don't like you at all.

Cerberus: Not everyone can be Heracles.

Heracles: If you at least pretended to be a normal dog. I suppose you wouldn't be very popular with the females.

At this point Heracles stopped talking—he had touched on a delicate subject. On the road they had passed female dogs, but Cerberus paid no attention to them.

Cerberus: If you had lived like me among decaying bodies, you would lose appetite for everything.

Heracles: Why do you eat grass and smell flowers, but you don't hunt rabbits? It makes no sense. Maybe you could howl. Do you remember our first night under an oak tree? Lord how time is flying; you howled beautifully.

Cerberus: How could I howl now? What did you tame me for?

Heracles: Mongrel, every idiot knows how to speak. You must howl, do you understand?

Cerberus: I won't howl.

Heracles: Well then, sleep.

Heracles thought feverishly: this absurd relationship has to be broken. When King Eurystheus sees Cerberus, he will notice right away he is not a threatening figure but comical. He will find one more labor for me, while people will see for themselves that life after death has completely . . . gone to hell. What, then, will become of the fashion of death, of its discrete presence so full of insinuations?

Dawn. Heracles and Cerberus wake simultaneously, as if their sleep and waking are tied by a common thread.

Heracles: Listen, I haven't made any sacrifices for a long time, and it is because of you.

Cerberus: Why because of me?

Heracles: I have to guard you.

Cerberus: It's nice of you.

Heracles: Not at all. I am neglecting my religious duties. Do you see that temple in the distance?

Cerberus: I don't see very well; so many years in the darkness. . . .

Heracles: Don't feel sorry for yourself. The temple is far away, I will reach it by sunset. Tomorrow at dawn I will make a sacrifice, and I will return at midnight, maybe later. Stay here and keep watch; don't budge from the spot. I don't want to have to search for you, is it clear?

Cerberus: I will keep watch.

Heracles ran blindly ahead. Sometimes he stopped and looked, listening, peering anxiously behind. He weaved as he ran, changing directions, walking against the wind, wading through marshes and streams to lose his tracks. He wanted to obliterate that stubborn smell of a master and his dog that clings to each blade of grass, each sand grain, and is immediately recognized by every four-legged creature as a unique, peculiar, divine odor.

Well, one can flee not only from an enemy but also from a

burden of attachment. Everyone does it, or knows the temptation very well.

At dusk Heracles made a sleeping place in the branches of an old elm. When he fell asleep he was on a tower, beyond the sphere of apprehension.

In the morning, two pairs of eyes were watching every movement of the awakened man.

They continued their journey. But can one call a journey an unrelenting chase to a destination at the limits of a human's and a dog's heart?

They stopped only briefly for the night or meals. Heracles was bored and decided to give Cerberus some lessons on natural history, taking the latest scientific discoveries into account.

A partisan of the descriptive method, he thrust his hand into grass as if into green water.

—You see, this is *Trifolium pratense*, popularly known as clover. It grows in meadows; its perennial root is spindle-shaped and bifurcating. Papyli grow on delicate, hairy offshoots. They contain bacteria that assimilate azote (like all plants in the Papilionaecae family). Its flowers are light red or dark scarlet. They have round heads, surrounded at the base by leaves.

He rummaged in the grass again and pulled out an oval, red object.

—Here is *Dorcus parallelopidens*. It is voracious. It lives in deciduous forests. The larvae develop in rotten oaks and beeches. Are you following me?

Tomorrow we will speak about photosynthesis and the early work by Kant, *Allgemeine Naturgeschichte und Theorie des Himmels*. Now go to sleep, blockhead.

They reached Mycenae the next evening. The city was deserted. It was close to autumn and a cold, stubborn drizzle was drifting down. They walked through empty streets, along walls the color of liver; Heracles walked in front, with difficulty assuming the look of a victor. Behind him Cerberus, content with himself, idiotically happy, tried to walk in step like an obedient recruit.

Not a trace of a triumphal entrance. Yet it was an unusually dramatic event that happened only once in the world's history—it deserved a wreath, applauding crowds, trumpets and pealing bells.

From beginning to end a worm had been gnawing at this beautiful flower of victory, and the severest fate—the fate of banality—hovered over the hero. It stripped away all glory and flattened everything, pushing a beautiful deed low, very low, into the realm of the anecdote.

When he was fighting his way through rain and mud with his freakish monster, it might have been a consolation for Heracles to know that King Eurystheus was watching him from his palace window with growing alarm.

Cerberus went berserk. In all his life he had never seen so many people smelling of wine and garlic; he terrorized the vegetable markets, devouring countless quantities of cauliflowers, artichokes, and cucumbers, and rampaged among market stands smelling of celery, frightening the vendors. Children adored him and rode on his back.

King Eurystheus did not want to see either Heracles or Cerberus. He asked them to leave the city.

—Mongrel, Heracles said, I am bored by this constant, hungry wandering from town to town. We should start a circus. You will walk on your hind legs in front of the gaping spectators, I will threaten you and crack my whip. Do you know how to walk on your hind legs?

—Of course, said Cerberus, a little bit hurt. He liked the idea.

One day Heracles brought a gray hemp sack from a nearby town. He casually mentioned to Cerberus that he would sleep on it because his bones ached from sleeping on the bare ground. Cerberus accepted this unquestioningly. The thought didn't dawn in either of his two heads that the tragic finale of the whole story was approaching.

The nagging question will remain unanswered forever, how could Heracles push this damp, dirty sack deep into the dark opening full of helpless screams and the howling of disappointed love.

Eos

—Do we have to? asks Eurydice. Hermes smiles, he is silent. As they walk, darkness parts before them and immediately closes after them. They pass through count-less gates.

—Is it necessary? asks Eurydice. Orpheus is old, I won't live with him much longer. I have forgotten the herbs I used for his throat which was sore from singing. I have forgotten what it is to get up at dawn. Or what a man wants when he touches my belly.

—Your memory will come back, Hermes says, gently and without conviction.

—You want to cheer me up, says Eurydice.

The road goes uphill, it is not a road but an obedient parting of cliffs. Flints smell like dried lightning. The small pebbles underfoot have completely forgotten the sea.

—Does he see us? Eurydice asks with concern.

With a motion of his head, Hermes denies it.

—I see his back. Always, when I was alive, I was moved by a man's back; it is helpless. But I don't feel this any longer. Tenderness—what is tenderness?

—The joy of touch, Hermes answers, a kind of lower ecstasy.

—My fingers are no longer alive, complains Eurydice. I couldn't thread a needle or remove a mote from the eye of someone I loved.

One more turn and the descent begins. Darkness, as if slanted, leaning over another deeper darkness.

—Eurydice, Hermes says in a low voice, I will reveal the secret of your fate. Orpheus will soon die in suspicious circumstances. You will be free and take as husband a healthy athlete with shoulders like the branches of an oak. He will be a young man, without imagination, wise enough not to desire unattainable things. You can't imagine how invigorating it will be after a life with a talented crybaby.

—I think, Eurydice says quickly, they would stone me to death rather than permit a second marriage. I will become a national widow, an advertisement for faithfulness and poetry. They will put me on a cliff where I am supposed to mutter inspired prophecies, or imprison me in a temple, which amounts to the same thing. Then I will die for a second time. How does one die a second time? I hope it isn't as painful and difficult as the first.

Orpheus hears all of this through the pouring darkness. For the first time he admires Eurydice's wisdom. Is it really necessary to die in order to become an adult?

A basalt landscape opens before him, as stately as a burnt forest, motionless as the eye of a volcano or the inside of thick matter. Azure of night burnt by nothingness.

> I sang dawns the coronations of the sun
> the journey of colors from morning to evening
> but I forgot about you
> > eternal night

Orpheus suddenly turns toward the shadows of Eurydice and Hermes and shouts in rapture—I've found it!

The shadows disappear. Orpheus comes into the light of day. He bursts with joyful pride that he has experienced a revelation, and discovered a new kind of literature, called, from now on, the poetry of reflection and darkness.

The King of the Ants

Ajax was the son of Zeus and Aegina, who was a river god's daughter. He was born on a deserted island. As he grew in years, he had the vague conviction that somehow he was sole ruler of this empty piece of earth in the immensity of waters: both ruler and exile at the same time. Like most foundlings, he had no idea who his father was. But he preserved a hazy memory of his mother, and he baptized the island with her name.

In the beginning, then, there was a name, a wasteland, and a king.

Ajax's only occupation was solemn idleness. This is the privilege of rulers, in the final analysis, even their duty—the manifestation of a frozen existence, a vigilant presence either benevolent or menacing. But for this one needs someone else's eyes or mirrors, because in emptiness each hieratic fold, each gesture, each lordly look turns into nothing. He was not endowed with the abilities of a Robinson Crusoe (who with such enthusiasm and praiseworthy results remade the entire practical manual of civilization), so Ajax invented an occupation and called it to himself "the royal inspection of the estate."

For entire days he wandered across the island in burned grass, rare trees, bushes, and timidly gurgling springs, their waters sinking in stone and disappearing in sand as if it never occurred to them they could at least be the beginning of a meager stream. Vegetation was sparse, there were almost no animals except a few families of frightened hares. On the other hand, there was an abundance of insects: whole swarms of crickets, beetles, and ants, the rustling of wing cases and the noise of their crawling forming an undergrowth of what we call the symphony of creation.

On clear nights Ajax set out toward a small bay and until dawn stared at the sensational Nereids dancing in somewhat decadent moonlight, at the herds of dolphins and seals coming to shore, all swinging as if they still carried the slippery sphere of the ocean on their backs. He envied them, he even envied the schools of fish because his longing for a community was inconsolable.

At dawn he returned, even more lonely, to his palace—a violet shadow under an oak—and prayed for the father of the gods to send people to him. He fervently swore he would be understanding and good to them.

Zeus took pity on his abandoned son. In a dream Ajax saw how ants fell like red dew from the leaves and branches of the oak under which he slept, and as they touched the earth they were transformed into human shapes. When he woke the island was teeming with them. Voices drifted in the air, comings and goings, a marvelous confusion.

So instead of just a single pair salvaged from Noah's ark, a sizable chunk of humanity was bestowed on Ajax as a gift. There were hard-to-define creatures as well, of both genders, like algae crushed by sterility or the absurdity of life: long-haired youths who stared vacantly into the distance instead of doing anything positive, signifying they were studying the philosophy of the Far East; grown men and women with gentle and expressionless faces, unclassical noses, thick limbs; finally old women suffering from rheumatism who dropped everything from their hands; and old men, some garrulous, some gloomy, for whom the only consolation before death was that the world had gone insane forever. In a word Ajax had humanity just as it should be: incorrigible in an exemplary way, marvelously ordinary.

The pious king called the new inhabitants of the island Myrmidons—the people of ants. In this way he wanted to glorify the goodness of the god and his miraculous intervention. How could he know that the name contained a destiny?

The fundamental duty of a good ruler is to learn the personality of his subjects: their merits and defects, the particular shape of their way of thinking and their yearnings. So Ajax assiduously observed the Myrmidons' customs. He tried to reach into the hidden nooks and crannies of their collective consciousness with all his sympathy, but sometimes also with carefully concealed anxiety and surprise.

The Myrmidons possessed an instinctive ability for self-organization rarely encountered in other peoples. They embarked on activities spontaneously, voluntarily, like children beginning a game. The division of labor presented no difficulties, everything was carried out without supervisors, overseers, prompters, the least trace of administration or hierarchy. They simply worked harmoniously from dawn till night, with a certain Protestant exaggeration, inspired, not counting on admiration or praise.

Historians of civilization, ethnologists, and structuralists carefully avoid the subject of the Myrmidons, because they do not fit their simple tripartite schemes. In the case of this peculiar people, banished from scientific textbooks, doctoral dissertations and international symposia, it was uncertain what was sacred and what profane, what was the top and the bottom, good and evil, or how the thesis—always fiercely fighting the antithesis—could be crowned with a salutary synthesis in the end.

It is true the Myrmidons were not distinguished by inquisitiveness, or excess of imagination. Their religion, surprisingly monotheistic, was limited to the old Pelasgian cult of the Mother Goat. In the domain of morality they stood in the middle, between the exuberance of virtues and the quagmire of vice. The time-honored custom of settling accounts with one's neighbor—or brother—by methodically hitting his skull with a rock was alien to them, also theft, false testimony, and calumny. Adultery was committed only by persons suffering from temporary amnesia.

The Myrmidons firmly rejected all styles of architecture. They built their settlements underground. These consisted of an intricate system of corridors, dark squares, and chambers. The advantages were that a fire department was superfluous, and the natural environment was preserved. Above all they loudly praised the attractions of the underground climate, its pleasant coolness, independence from the capriciousness of weather, and invigorating sleep under the power of roots—sleep without starry prophecies or nightmares, tightly filled with loam, clay, and sand. They were psychologically well balanced. During their long history it is difficult to meet even a single person touched, for instance, by religious mania.

Science is mute about the Myrmidons' methods of work, but these are worthy of attention, different from known models and completely their own. The Myrmidons put their entire trust in handicrafts, in the literal sense; they rejected the comfort of tools, the benefit of the wheel, the pulley and simple lever.

Armed simply with sharpened poles and sticks, they cultivated their poor fields and vegetable gardens as the pitiless sun destroyed the fruits of their labor. They built roads and canals that were constantly buried by sand, they spent laborious months on eternal repairs of underground settlements that collapsed over their heads. The installation of a tiny footbridge (for a beaver with average education, it would be like eating breakfast) was a gigantic enterprise for the Myrmidons that passed from one generation to another.

However, they never lost enthusiasm, energy, and a sense of well-being. Progress—that treacherous force that pushes humanity toward risky extravaganzas—suffered. On the other hand, full employment provided a sense of security.

They always worked together, and it always seemed there were too many of them. They struggled with resistant matter. Although the results were not imposing, one could not take one's eyes away from those strained muscles, bent backs, and living hands struggling with the soulless mass. The acoustic effects accompanying these efforts were worthy of the highest admiration. Loud youthful calls, songlike mutual encouragement, rhythmic sounds coming from the depths of the lungs, cries of triumph and defeat—all these composed a cantata of rare beauty. Toothless old men always gathered next to those who were working, increasing a confusion already considerable as they commented in a lively way on the exploits of the working teams, giving loud advice and stern reprimands.

Such were the Myrmidons.

The fate of Ajax was worthy of envy. He was loved by the gods and by his subjects. It would seem that the idylls imagined by the dreamer Plato and the dreamer Vladimir Ilych were realized in perfect form. In addition they were based not on theory or conviction—which, after all, are changeable—but on the stable foundation of genetics.

New, almost revolutionary ideas sprouted in the king's head. He wanted to give his people autonomy, then slowly to transfer different spheres of power to them, limiting his own functions to representation, to preaching occasional sermons and conjuring rain. Here he met with the Myrmidons' resistance, passive and decided. They pleaded that they had enough of their own domestic occupations. Nor did they have enthusiasm for the titles (inexpensive things, and generally desired) that he wanted to bestow on certain citizens. These were supposed to lead to the formation of a generic aristocracy, and, in turn, to fruitful social tension. The king continued to reside under the oak tree, so the title of Court Chamberlain meant as much as Chamberlain of a shadow.

Because of the functions he performed and also because of his temperament, Ajax was a conservative but an enlightened conservative. He realized that an undisturbed harmony between ruler and subjects contradicts the laws of nature, therefore one had to go out and meet halfway those changes that are inevitable, even lure them out of the dark nooks of fate in order to tame them more easily later on.

He initiated cautious reforms, starting neither with the base nor with the superstructure (according to the genial distinction of the scholar Jotvues), but with linguistic innovations.

On a hot July day, a ceremonial meeting of all the inhabitants took place. The king declared that from now to eternity, Aegina would be called Myrmidonia in honor of its brave citizens. In this way he wanted to waken a dormant sense of national pride and uniqueness: to liberate man's incomprehensible tendency to elevate himself above others for rather insignificant reasons—place of birth, skin pigmentation, the shape of the nose. He also decided that the main road—a path, strictly speaking—running in the middle of the island would bear the name Avenue of Victory.

The Myrmidons received these ordinances calmly, shaking their heads. But everything remained as it was, the old way. In a quarrel about universals, the meek inhabitants, without realizing it, took the position of those who claim that general concepts are inherent in things and do not float like menacing clouds over objects. Such was their simplicity.

The education of society, like all education, implies a gradation, passing from easier degrees to the more difficult. After his first defeat, Ajax initiated the next stage of national education. In order to prepare his stubborn provincials to meet other peoples, he announced that an International Trade Fair would soon take place on the island.

A number of merchants, mostly from Crete, came to Aegina. The Myrmidons exhibited the best they had to offer: sticks for farming, shoes made of bark, homespun jackets, clay pots without decoration, hemp string with knots that passed for jewelry. The guests, however, glittered with the dazzling wealth of their exhibits: their proverbial beads and percales, new automatic models of plows, objects for killing animals and people, pendants, earrings, feather diadems, and merchandise the purpose of which the inhabitants of Aegina could not even guess.

All this was looked at without great interest; the consumer's instinct didn't even budge. A scandal was caused by their total lack of understanding for articles that everywhere else enjoyed great popularity: namely pitchers, amphoras, and mixing bowls on which the best painters of the period depicted gods, animals, and people in intimate situations, representing them with minute, detailed realism.

Soon after the merchants' visit that ended in a fiasco, rich deposits of silver were accidentally discovered on the island. Ajax immediately understood that this was a gift from the gods: it might lift Aegina out of its backwardness, permit a leap from a primitive barter economy to the exchange of money, and awaken the desire to possess. Finally, it could divide the monotonously homogeneous inhabitants into the fat and the lean, the rich and the poor. But the incorrigible Myrmidons broke the precious metal against rocks, changing it into powder which they scattered on the corridors of their underground dwellings.

The king was not discouraged by setbacks. When someone firmly sets his mind to make humanity happy, it is difficult, unfortunately, to dissuade him. Ajax knew that happiness implies movement, striving, climbing upward. But he did not know that progress, to use this ominous word, was only an image, neither better nor worse than other figments of the imagination. On the other hand the Myrmidons, who were deprived of imagination and never expressed their thoughts (their convictions were stronger because of it), knew as a certainty that life is a circle bound by death. It is closed rather than open, individual rather than general, contained exactly within the limits of every separate body: of men, of insects, of trees. This is why naked feet walking in a circle are more natural than a march following in the steps of a dreadful giant who triumphantly strides toward goals hidden behind the horizon, along a straight line that comes from nothing and leads to a better, radiant nothing.

After his unsuccessful experiments in basis and language, Ajax decided to attack the problem of the embarrassing apathy of his subjects from the direction of superstructure. To be sure, the intellectual standard of an average Myrmidon left much to be desired. No one was attracted by learning, or even theology. They took the world as it was (naive realism) and considered questioning it a waste of time.

Ajax started to bring to the island the most eminent philosophers from the continent. They were to speak about everything that came into their heads, exactly like the present practice in universities of the Western hemisphere. The undertaking was planned on a huge scale and was to last for years; the participation of citizens was obligatory and included women, children, even infants.

This time the ruler's initiative met with a response that surpassed all expectations, filling the royal heart with boundless joy. The Myrmidons went to the lectures in crowds, even without special incentives. They sat in a large semicircle around the speaker, closing their eyes, some opening their mouths, while others rested their heads on their hands, filled with metaphysical revery. Silence reigned, interrupted only by an occasional deep sigh.

Until one day it exploded. When a speaker finished his lecture with a fundamental statement expressing the ontological principle of identity—"it is necessary to say and to think that what is exists, because existence is, and nonexistence is not"—a burst of laughter as powerful as thunder could be heard.

It was not at all a scoffing laughter but an explosion of spontaneous, unrestrained joy. The Myrmidons rolled on the ground, bellowed, chuckled, those who lost their breath made whining squeaks and yelps like a dog. They beat their heads with their hands, and tears of pure happiness flowed from their eyes.

After this incident, philosophers stopped visiting Aegina. What is more, the name Myrmidons became—how unjustly—synonymous with spiritual coarseness. Yet no one but they made the momentous discovery that every intellectual labor is a peculiar degeneration, and its results contain a powerful dose of the comic. Invented problems, intellectual constructions, categories and concepts—if one looks at them closely—are irresistibly funny. Of all the wisdom bestowed on the Myrmidons, they accepted in their colloquial language only the word *apeiron*. For philosophers, it designates infinity. The Myrmidons endowed it with their own meaning that designated all superfluous things such as trash, bones licked clean, and tornadoes.

One can evaluate Ajax's attempts at reform in many different ways, but they created a new situation. Aegina took leave of its weightless state and finally entered Greek topography. This is probably why it started to attract peculiar visitors.

These were young people whose business, to speak in the most general way, was transportation: the transportation of ideas, by sea and by land.

Like the philosophers, they had the not very tactful habit of teaching others how to live. But unlike the philosophers, they did it in a more direct way, without intellectual intricacies, and sometimes quite violently. They taught the Myrmidons that everything important and essential takes place in one's head—that is, in an imaginary world—and that this world is stronger than the visible world. They also explained to the Myrmidons how miserable they were. The measure of their misfortune was the fact that they did not realize it at all. The main cause of their misery was their incompetent, weak government. Ajax should be thrown out and democracy introduced.

The Myrmidons, however, were unanimously content with their life. Why, then, should they throw out their gentle king? They showed total lack of interest in democracy because with typical, naive sincerity, they admitted they didn't know what it meant. It is possible, they said, the world tended in this direction, but why should they, the Myrmidons, be like the world instead of like themselves?

According to the holy principles of theory, revolutions are always carried out from "the bottom." In completely exceptional cases it is possible to contrive them from the top. This is of course a deviation, and as such should be carefully passed over in silence. Once everything is arranged, one must quickly invent a genesis, background, and chronology according to the principles of science. The transporters started secret negotiations with Ajax. They highly praised his desires for reforms, but—he had to admit it himself—he hadn't achieved much. To lead the Myrmidons out of their backwardness, dramatic methods had to be used. Bloodshed was necessary.

This word reappeared many times, in each conversation. Poor Ajax trembled all over, he grew pale, sometimes even wept. With all the gods as his witnesses, he swore nothing was as foreign to him as violence, and that he would never allow any harm to be done to the inhabitants of the island. They answered that during truly unpleasant events he would be removed behind a curtain. The king grew pale, whimpered, and softened.

It is difficult to pass in silence over an obvious question: Why did Ajax agree to these conversations? They became a source of psychological torture for him. He was a free man, he could simply show his uninvited guests to the door: that is, beyond the perimeter of the shadowy oak tree.

The simple explanation of this enigma can be found in a strange trait in the nature of men. Instead of shrugging their shoulders, they consider it their sacred duty to answer idiotic questions and arrogant provocations, becoming in this way easy prey for various madmen. The dividing line between an accidental situation and a relationship lasting an entire life is very fluid; married couples know about this. It is possible to avoid many unpleasant occurrences, even catastrophes, by summoning the aid of common sense.

But this is an extremely rare spiritual virtue, particularly among thinking, delicate individuals. Almost everyone carries inside him a vague sense of guilt, and from this guilt our neighbor, if he is a bit clever, can concoct dangerous things. Ajax considered himself a weak ruler, and in addition one who did not sufficiently love his subjects. The transporters knew it well. This knowledge was enough to undermine Ajax's psychological structure: metaphorically speaking, to conquer the fortress.

The transporters worked out a scenario and presented it to the king for his approval. It was simple (let us honor this subtlety). At a designated moment a kind of simulated coup would take place with all the appearances of being real. Ajax would be slightly wounded, and—this was planned beforehand—carried behind the curtains. A few Myrmidons would be accused of an attempt at regicide. During a public trial they would receive stiff punishment. At that moment the inhabitants of the island would naturally divide into supporters and adversaries of the coup; this would be the beginning of a productive antagonism. From then on affairs would proceed according to the laws of dialectics, from good forms to better and better forms, until in the end the butterfly of perfection would take flight from its gray cocoon.

Indeed it almost happened. It is the Myrmidons, one must sadly admit, who with their inexcusable stubbornness and dullness bear the historical blame for causing the butterfly's death. Quite simply, none of those who were accused admitted their guilt. This sentence should be repeated several times, because it sounds absolutely fantastic. The gentle persuasions of the transporters, and their sophisticated tortures, came to nothing.

In their fierce stubbornness the Myrmidons said that to lift a stone, one first has to want to lift the stone (in other words, to kill a king one has to want to). Everyone knew that they loved their ruler, and what man of healthy mind would freely deprive himself, with his own free will, of the object of his love? They were not convinced by the argument that Ajax intended to sacrifice his life on the altar of a better future, because he had never talked about the topic. In fact nobody, not even a rabbit, wants to be killed. (Parenthetically, let us notice the primitive quality of the metaphors of the Myrmidons: a stone, a rabbit).

The accused were confirmed in their conviction that the king was no longer there. He had left for a better world; their resistance was useless, they were fighting for a shadow. But the Myrmidons, who knew the real value of shadow, defended themselves with the determination that comes from despair. Intellectually backward, they rejected without deeper reflection the argument that they did not want the murder subjectively, but objectively they did. This sophism, invented by semi-intellectuals with political inclinations, is older than it seems. In addition, the accused repeatedly asked their torturers how it was possible to sleep next to one's wife (this was exactly their case) and at the same time plot something in a distant location. (The principle of the excluded middle, moral rather than logical, undermined or enlarged by polyvalent logic that luckily had not been invented.)

Bitterness, revulsion, and spite filled the transporters' hearts to such an extent that they decided to end their mission and abandon the island. To leave behind at least a small trace of their visit, they killed all those who were accused, without exception. This was supposed to mean that the ax was buried, but they would return at the first call of history.

The Myrmidons celebrated the restoration of monarchy in an atmosphere of unusual enthusiasm. What is strange is that Ajax returned in glory. If it was possible, he was loved even more ardently than before the short invasion. He tried to explain and justify himself. No one wanted to listen to him.

His sensitive conscience did not leave him in peace. He seemed to look at his subjects sadly, because nobody blamed him for anything. For him, their trust was a reproach, their total devotion a burden. So he asked his heavenly father to call him away from this mystic island where goodness was natural, evil came always from outside, and nothing—absolutely nothing—was in between.

For the second time, Zeus took pity on his son. He nominated him for a managerial position in the Department of Justice of the afterlife.

In the heat of narration we have forgotten to mention that Ajax was married twice and from each marriage had a son. Both boys, or rather men, were exceptionally handsome. It is difficult to say anything about their other merits. Only later did it turn out that they were unscrupulous, a trait in individuals who try to compensate for inborn dullness with an excess of ambition.

Here we suspend our tale, because just at this moment Clio enters the holy grove of myth: a big girl, tall, clumsy, strong as a horse, and coarse beyond words—the goddess of usurpers, repeating her worn-out clichés.

ZBIGNIEW HERBERT (1924–1998) was a spiritual leader of the anticommunist movement in Poland. His work has been translated into almost every European language; he has won numerous prizes, most recently the Jerusalem Prize and the T. S. Eliot Prize. His books include *Selected Poems*, *Report from the Besieged City and Other Poems*, *Mr. Cogito*, *Still Life with a Bridle*, and the new *Elegy for the Departure and Other Poems*, all available from The Ecco Press.

JOHN AND BOGDANA CARPENTER, longtime Herbert translators, won the PEN Translation Award for his *Selected Poems*. John Carpenter is a poet and a critic; Bogdana Carpenter is a professor of Slavic Languages and Literature at the University of Michigan. They live in Ann Arbor, Michigan.